MW01094036

Tales from Kentucky Funeral Homes

Best wishes to
Trudy Craft, who is
not yet ready for funeral
service!

Lynwood Montell,
author
10/12/19

TALES FROM
KENTUCKY
FUNERAL HOMES

William Lynwood Montell

THE UNIVERSITY PRESS OF KENTUCKY

Scholarly publisher for the Commonwealth,
serving Bellarmine University, Berea College, Centre
College of Kentucky, Eastern Kentucky University,
The Filson Historical Society, Georgetown College,
Kentucky Historical Society, Kentucky State University,
Morehead State University, Murray State University,
Northern Kentucky University, Transylvania University,
University of Kentucky, University of Louisville,
and Western Kentucky University.

Editorial and Sales Offices: The University Press of Kentucky
663 South Limestone Street, Lexington, Kentucky 40508–4008
www.kentuckypress.com

The Library of Congress has cataloged the hardcover edition as follows:

Montell, William Lynwood, 1931–
Tales from Kentucky funeral homes / William Lynwood Montell.
    p.   cm.
ISBN 978-0-8131-2567-1 (hardcover : alk. paper)
1. Undertakers and undertaking—Kentucky—Anecdotes. 2. Funeral
rites and ceremonies—Kentucky—Anecdotes. 3. Death—Social
aspects—Kentucky—Anecdotes. 4. Kentucky—Social life and
customs—Anecdotes. I. Title.
HD9999.U53K46   2009
395.2'309769—dc22
                            2009018240

ISBN 978-0-8131-6823-4 (pbk. : alk. paper)
ISBN 978-0-8131-7361-0 (pdf)
ISBN 978-0-8131-3943-2 (epub)

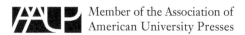

To all funeral directors who made this book possible and to my family: my wife, Linda; my children and their spouses—Monisa and Jack Wright, Brad and Marla Montell, and Lisa and Nick Adkins; my grandchildren—Frank, Alex, and Rob Wright, Tyler and Hunter Montell, Hannah Neighbors, and Zoe Adkins; and my great-grandson, Maverick Wright

CONTENTS

INTRODUCTION

~

As a folklorist, I have a long-standing interest in the importance of oral history, and during the early years of the twenty-first century I decided to record stories told by members of significant professional groups. The stories were published as *Tales from Kentucky Lawyers* (2003), *Tales from Tennessee Lawyers* (2005), and *Tales from Kentucky Doctors* (2008). I fully realized that funeral directors' accounts also held important historical content, since they are the final persons to care for friends and community members when death occurs. I have collected their stories here to preserve their memories and to document the funeral practices of earlier years and contemporary times.

I began the story-recording process in November 2007. Some funeral directors whom I asked to participate turned me down because of busy schedules or the fear of bringing back sad, mournful memories to persons who might read this book. A number of other directors promised to send me tape-recorded stories or e-mail accounts but never followed through. However, I was able to record personal interviews with many funeral directors throughout the Commonwealth, and these generous professionals willingly reminisced about their profession, their individual practices, and local burial customs across the years. Their stories are filled with interesting details, humorous anecdotes, and telling insights into human nature.

I had two criteria for making contacts with potential storytellers. First, they should typically be middle-aged or older, as they would likely have more interesting, memorable accounts to share, especially if they had ancestors who had founded family funeral homes. Second, they should be practitioners in small- to medium-size towns or cities located in all regions of Kentucky. Thanks to referrals and personal contacts made by funeral directors whom I interviewed, I was able to talk with practitioners in Symsonia, Owensboro, Lewisburg, Leitchfield, Morgantown, Bowling Green, Brownsville, Glasgow, Fountain Run, Tompkinsville, Summer Shade, Hardinsburg, Elizabethtown, Louisville, Bloomfield, Campbellsville, Shelbyville, Mt. Vernon, Irvine, Pineville, Morehead, and Ashland.

For most interviews, I met the funeral directors in their offices, waiting rooms, or actual homes and chatted for several minutes so we could get to know each other before the storytelling sessions began. Then I turned on the tape recorder and asked them why they'd chosen to become a funeral director, whether their ancestors had been in the business, and where they had worked and why. I also asked for stories in certain natural categories—funeral and burial customs, humorous incidents and mistakes, and the behavior of the bereaved, for example—which became the organizing points for the chapters in this collection.

After completing the recordings, I transcribed all the interviews and sent copies to the funeral directors, asking them to make any necessary additions, deletions, or corrections. Once I received their edited versions, I made all the requested revisions in my computer files. Thus, the stories in this book are verbatim accounts told by the storytellers.

The storytellers themselves are competent, licensed funeral directors, and their professional status adds authority to their narratives. Most accounts are about their personal experiences, sometimes beginning in their assistantship years, and about the practices of their parents and grandparents. Some feature other funeral directors, not relatives but professional acquaintances or friends of friends, local or scattered across the region. Virtually every account I include was told as a true personal experience or a story, passed along from person to person, of something that actually happened. Such stories are a significant source for persons conducting research about local life and culture and about the 99.9 percent of the world's population whose names never get into history books. The practice of recording these stories, as utilized in this book, represents a viable approach to historical documentation and forms the basis for oral history methodology.

Like many other professionals, funeral directors depend on one another to share information and pass along reliable accounts that will help them fulfill their important role in serving society. In fact, meaningful professional narratives are significant sources of professional education and support. In the words of anthropologist Elliott Oring,

"There is experimental evidence that shows that information conveyed in a narrative is better remembered, more persuasive, and engenders greater belief than statistical information communicated on the same topic."[1] Thus, when funeral directors share stories about events that really happened, they are helping one another and future generations of professionals to understand their history and how to do their work.

According to long-time funeral director Charles McMurtrey, "A funeral director is a person who has the responsibility to get a death certificate filled out and signed and sent to Frankfort. The owner of a funeral home has to be a licensed funeral director and a licensed embalmer. To me, the job of the funeral director is to take possession of the body, working out the arrangements and notifying newspapers and radios." These days, as in past times, lineal descendants must be notified as soon as death occurs. In early times, notification was sent by sad letters edged in black, but in the more recent past, telephones, telegraphs, and radio and television stations provided news about local deaths. Even today, as soon as news of a death breaks, it is typical to call the local funeral director in change of the visitation and burial process to obtain needed information. Funeral directors must also explain to bereaved families and the public what happens at the funeral home. Their explanatory accounts deal with the reality of human experience and enhance their professional standing in the community.

The foreword of *Gone to Glory . . . Here's the Story: Undertaking Tales from Tennessee* describes the role of funerals in our culture: "Funerals are the American way of saying goodbye. Although goodbyes are never easy, they are essential to both our health and well-being. The American funeral also keeps us tied to our past. For centuries families have gathered at the death of a loved one only to be reacquainted with relatives that have remained unseen. We greet each other with a hug and wonder why it has been so long. We then begin to reminisce about past days, and how wonderful life was way back when. Our short time together is filled with interesting stories and anecdotes that keep our past alive and well, even when the details have been blurred by time. When the funeral is over we make promises of getting together sometime, only to find that sometime will bring another funeral."[2]

Dying is a family affair in the American South, as it is in other portions of the United States, and each subculture has its traditions. In larger cities across Kentucky, for example, funeral homes owned by African American funeral directors have been in existence for many years and have followed parental and ancestral practices. An unpublished article written by Erich March, graduate of Johns Hopkins University and vice president of March Funeral Homes in Baltimore, Maryland, contains the following meaningful commentary: "The tradition of the 'Home-Going Service' when used to characterize and memorialize the passing of a loved one, is no less unique as a funeral ritual when caring for the dead in the black community. . . . To slaves, death was not viewed as an act of dying, but as an act of 'Going Home.' . . . We must remember that ancient Egypt was an African country ruled by an African people and all historians give them credit for developing the techniques of embalming and preparing the deceased for ritual services. The act of preserving a deceased human being in order to conduct funeral services over an extended period of time and placing them in a container for burial is practiced all over the world as a way of remembering the life of a loved one. This method of commemoration was started by a people of color."[3]

In any community, laughter and humor may be an important part of condoling with bereaved families and friends. Humorous stories are also a part of funeral directors' professional and social get-togethers. Whether humorous or sad, the stories in this book are based on real happenings experienced by funeral director storytellers throughout Kentucky. I truly enjoyed recording their stories and their viewpoints about the funeral profession across the years. Were it not for collections like this, the historically significant stories of professional groups such as funeral directors, lawyers, doctors, and others would not be preserved for future generations to read and appreciate.

Notes

1. Elliott Oring, "Legendry and the Rhetoric of Truth," *Journal of American Folklore* 121 (Spring 2008), 145.

2. Robert W. Batson, *Gone to Glory…Here's the Story: Undertaking Tales from Tennessee* (Tennessee Funeral Directors Association, 2003), i.

3. Erich March, "The History of the African-American Funeral Service: Our 'Home-Going' Heritage," provided by Gayle Graham, funeral director at W. T. Shumake and Daughters Funeral Home, Louisville, KY.

1

FUNERAL AND BURIAL PRACTICES THROUGH THE YEARS

~

In the days before electricity and indoor plumbing, many families lacked the money to pay for funeral expenses; but funeral directors understood and were willing to wait until payment came later on. People used horse-drawn hearses and handmade caskets (also known as coffins and burial boxes) made by the deceased prior to need. Early embalming often took place at home, which required putting the body fluids into buckets. Sons sometimes helped their funeral-director fathers prepare for funeral services and burials. Bereaved family members were also allowed to help with the embalming process.

It was typical in early times to use horses to pick up bodies located in remote areas, and even after the coming of funeral hearses, horses were at times used to pull the hearses/ambulances along muddy roads and across hills in order to reach the appropriate cemetery. In one of the following tales, a one-horse "ambulance" pulled a sled through the woods with a body on it. Ambulance runs for the sick and deceased were performed by virtually all funeral homes until the 1970s.

Whether the funeral service was conducted at the funeral home or in a church, there was singing that paid tribute to the deceased, a message by one or more ministers, and then additional singing while friends and community members passed slowly by the casket to pay final respects to the deceased. When the onlookers had gone by, family members moved in closely to take a final look at the departed loved one and perhaps to leave a kiss or caress before the funeral director closed the lid.

AMBULANCE AND DEATH CALLS

During the early years of having ambulance service in the county, some people would call and ask for the ambulance to be sent, but in their excitement they would not identify themselves nor where the ambulance should go to.

The same thing would happen with death calls. The phone would ring and a voice would say, "Daddy passed away (or died). We want you all to come and get him. Our house will be the one with the light on the porch."

That worked pretty well, as we could make a good guess because that might be the only light on that road. But later on when everybody had electricity, and everyone had lights on that road, our strategy was to drive until we saw which house on that road had the most cars out front.

Word spreads fast in communities, and people are very close. Family and friends gather around when trouble comes.

James M. Pendley, Morgantown, March 3, 2008

SAD TIMES

There's not a whole lot of excitement in the funeral business. We just hope we are doing good jobs, and will continue to do so, in order to help families get through one of the worst days of their lives.

Funerals are sometimes social events. Even though it's a sad time, it is still a social event that brings family and community members together for the first time in years.

William Fields, Ashland, May 7, 2008

CHANGING TERMS

Terms have changed over the years. At one time, they called us undertakers; then they called us funeral directors; then they called us funeral directors and embalmers; and if they really wanted to get fancy, they called us morticians. So, we answered to anybody about anything. I personally am both a funeral director and embalmer. However, here in Kentucky, you can be just a funeral director and not a licensed embalmer, and you can be an embalmer and not a funeral director. In some states, you have to be both.

Terry Dabney, Campbellsville, October 13, 2007

Horse-Drawn Hearse

Back in my father's time he would go to the home of the dead person in a horse-drawn hearse as the means of hauling the body to and from the funeral home. Any transportation had to be done in this hearse. I remember that. Of course, it was waterproof and rain wouldn't bother anything. He had a good team to pull the hearse, and he would bring the body here to the funeral home and put it in a casket.

The family would come in and make arrangements as to where the burial was to take place.

Charles McMurtrey, Summer Shade, July 29, 2007

Back Then

Back then, they took a lot of bodies to the homes of the deceased and laid them out there. You had to have all kinds of equipment, such as a drape set, candelabra or cosmetic electric lamps, which were electric lights, one of which was put at the head of the casket and one at the foot. We also had a register stand back then. But all of these things broke down into cases, and you had to take all these things, along with chairs, fans, etc., to the house.

Billy Dowell, Mt. Vernon, August 27, 2007

Funeral Costs Back Then

It is said that the cost of a funeral in the nineteenth century was around two dollars! The cheapest funeral on our records here at what is now Hughes Funeral Home took place in 1928. It was sixty dollars. Many could not afford the services of a funeral director, and they paid with a promissory note and then made cash payments, or sometimes they paid with chickens or goats.

Connie Hughes Goodman, Fountain Run, September 11, 2007

Ambulance Service Too

Only funeral service homes provided ambulance service at one time. Funeral homes typically charged about five dollars for a local ambulance service request. In other words, the ambulance was used to pick a person up and take him or her to the hospital. That was back in the good old days, as five dollars wouldn't buy the gasoline today.

There are different charges for ambulance service runs today . . . but I'm not that familiar with it now, since we quit providing ambulance service and no longer have that headache!

William Fields, Ashland, May 7, 2008

BURYING BODIES IN THE WOODS

Back then, funeral homes were in ambulance work as well. They were the only ones that had a wagon big enough to haul a body. Of course, ambulances were ambulances, but we called them wagons! They were hearses. Some of them had tops on them, but some didn't have. The ones that had tops were big enough to haul a body in. And if somebody was real bad sick, we'd put a bed in that, put the sick person on it, and haul them like that.

We have been far enough back in the woods, where people lived in cabins, that we had to take one horse because there wasn't room enough for two. Take one horse, and it would pull a sled, and we'd fix a bed on the sled and pull that sled through the woods with the body on it.

Sometimes we had to take hold of one end of the sled and pull it around tree stumps and bushes. Sometimes we hauled bodies to the graveyards that were back in the woods. We had to go right through the woods with them like that, but sometimes it would be in a wagon that we used to take bodies to the graveyard. But sometimes we'd have to have pallbearers carry the body. And in real backwoods uphill places, we'd have to have three sets of pallbearers to swap around while carrying the body so they wouldn't get tired.

Edward Dermitt, Leitchfield, August 29, 2007

CARRYING A DRUNK MAN TO THE AMBULANCE

When I was a middle-aged man, I started funeral work, and I remember on one occasion that this man had laid in his house. He'd been drunk, and somebody called telling us they needed an ambulance to come get this man. When I got down there, his feet were really swelled up real big as a head.

I thought, well what can I do, and how can I get this man up on top of the hill? So, I got him as comfortable as I could and then I throwed him up over my shoulder and carried him up over this hill, then put him in an ambulance and took him to the veterans hospital in Louisville.

The veterans hospital then cared for him in such a way he got able to get around. After that, he'd come by the funeral home to visit people.

Edward Dermitt, Leitchfield, August 29, 2007

JEEP AMBULANCE MIRED DOWN

We had a jeep for an ambulance part of the time. We didn't always have it, but we made an ambulance out of it and fixed it so we could put a cot in it. Back over on Nolin River next to Hart County, I was sent late one afternoon to go get somebody that was real sick.

I drove this jeep, and the ground was froze. I drove way back in the country next to Nolin River to get a sick, crippled woman. I picked her up and got to a place where the frozen road was getting so slick that it would break through. On one occasion, all four wheels on this jeep ambulance went down in the frozen ground. And when they went down like that, I couldn't get the wheels out, so I had to do something. Well, I chopped and done everything I could to put supports under the jeep to hold it up.

I couldn't get out of the sunken places, so I left the patient in the jeep and walked two miles to get a tractor to pull the jeep out.

Well, the funeral director had sent several people in cars all over everywhere in the back roads trying to find me. They didn't find me, so along about ten o' clock that night after I took this lady to the hospital, these men came looking for me. Then, they found me.

Edward Dermitt, Leitchfield, August 29, 2007

DYING ON THE ROAD

We ran into a lot of little things in direct funeral work that we'd have to do. Most of the work consisted of ambulance work, getting [people] out and in. One funeral home would compete with the other because it had better ambulance equipment.

The funeral homes stopped using the ambulance in funeral services in 1973. That year a law was passed that said they had to be people that were schooled in EMT and have tools and equipment to handle patients that couldn't be handled in funeral cars.

I've had people with their neck broke, and we had to prop their neck up good, and everything. Sometimes I would put splints on their arms when they'd break their arms. Well, sometimes they'd live, and sometimes they'd die. I've had them die on the road.

Edward Dermitt, Leitchfield, August 27, 2007

THE END OF AMBULANCE SERVICE

For many years we did ambulance service. For three years I worked when we still had ambulance service, but after that the city and the county took over. The county took over on January 1 at 12:00 AM, 1975. Our funeral home stopped service then. When that happened, Metcalfe County joined Barren County. And about that same time, most of the funeral homes statewide started easing out of the ambulance service. As I understand it, the funeral homes were glad to get out of the ambulance service. It was really a hard business to do.

I think the reason the funeral homes got involved in ambulance service in the first place was because they had the only means of transportation that was comfortable and closed in, even in the old days of horse and buggy, or even when we just had motorized funeral coaches or hearses in which they could put a stretcher or cot to transport people as a means of convenience. Then it just evolved to more of a good-will gesture. I know the charges that we did didn't come close to anything at all, and a lot of times it might be five dollars for an in-town run, seven to ten dollars if it was out in the county. If you used any oxygen, the charge was three extra dollars.

But all we did, mainly, was provide transportation and a little first aid. In the early days there weren't too many ways to advertise the funeral business tactfully, I guess. So most of it was then, and still is to this day, good will.

Follis Crow, Glasgow, December 11, 2007

MAN MADE HIS OWN CASKET

I knew somebody that, years ago, actually went into the dead person's home and helped along such lines as shaving the face, closing their eyes, and dressing their body. I still remember that we buried a man that did that.

And some people used to make their own coffin. We had a man that came in here one morning bright and early, and said, "Mr. Brown, can I make a casket? Can I build my own casket?"

I said, "Sure."

Then he said, "Well, whenever I bring it here, will you store it?"

I never had been asked that question before, and I said, "Well, yeah, I guess I will."

Anyway, I didn't think too much more about it, but that very afternoon he walked in and said, "I've got my casket out here. Where do you want it?"

So I said to myself, "Uhuh." I didn't know how long he's going to live. It was going to get in the way. Anyway, I told him where we were going to put it. Then I looked in it. It had his underwear and everything, [all] his clothes. He then said, "Whenever I die, I want to be buried the same day that I die. I don't want to be laid out."

I said, "Well, we'll do our best. I guess it'll depend on what time of day you die."

So he said, "That's the way I want it."

He died about two years after that, and it was back in the seventies. His family didn't find him until the middle of the afternoon, so we couldn't get him buried that same day because it was during the winter. We didn't embalm him because he didn't want to be embalmed. We had to take him down into Grayson County, so we made arrangements to bury him at Big Clifty. So, we took him down there at the appointed time to conduct a graveside service, etc. When we got there, we drafted a few pallbearers, because the handles on this casket were made out of rope.

Since he was a pretty good size man, he didn't realize that the casket wasn't quite big enough for him. Well, we got him in it, but it was full! We had to carry him a pretty good distance, and I was scared to death that the bottom of that casket was going to fall out before we got to the grave. But it didn't, and we made it. We got him in the ground!

Bob Brown, Elizabethtown, September 25, 2007

EARLY PAYNEVILLE PRACTICE

Mr. Sturgeon at Brandenburg started out as a funeral director back in earlier times. I don't think he did very much out in homes. He'd bring [the deceased] into the funeral home that was in Payneville. He said he'd do the embalming in the front room where they were laid out. It would all be done in one room, and they would put sheets down around the body to keep everything off the floor. Then, whenever they got through with the body, they'd put it in a casket and take the cooling board out, take the sheets out. Then it was time for a visit. Most of the funerals were in the church.

Bob Brown, Elizabethtown, September 25, 2007

HANDMADE CASKETS

Some people didn't have a casket, so they'd come here to the funeral home to buy a casket. Or, they could go to a town close to them where they kept caskets, like they kept harness and machinery parts that were used on a farm. It was horse-drawn equipment. You could buy a casket there, too.

And some people would plane lumber real good with a hand planer. It had a piece of metal in it. They'd plane this wood real slick to make it look good, then make a casket out of it. They made their own casket. Then we'd use that casket in which to bury the person.

It is interesting to note that the farther back in the country you got, people often used the word "coffin" instead of "casket." And a few people just called them "boxes." We'd cover the caskets with a cloth cover sometimes. We'd either tack it onto the casket or glue it on.

These homemade caskets also had lids and screws to use to firmly close the top.

Edward Dermit, Leitchfield, August 29, 2007

COFFINS TO CASKETS

Years ago, funeral homes were always associated with furniture operations, because funeral homes didn't have a lot of business. They would make caskets, or coffins, as they were called back then. However, technology and other matters have really changed over the years. But as the funeral homes got out of the furniture woodworking businesses, casket manufacturing became more prevalent. Occasionally you can still get some people that make their own caskets.

Rayfield Houghlin, Bloomfield, October 17, 2007

SELLING CASKETS

Everybody has a different way of waiting on families and the way to treat families when they are making funeral arrangements.

I've always taken families into the display room to explain the caskets to them, and then I leave. I think that's pretty well what all of us were trained to do. And you'll hear them talking amongst themselves and will hear the term coffin, box—just different terms when they are talking about the casket.

James M. Pendley, Morgantown, March 3, 2008

FURNITURE MAKERS AS FUNERAL DIRECTORS

Some of the funeral directors actually built the caskets they used in the funeral business. As a matter of fact, I guess some of the first funeral homes were located in furniture stores in the United States, because they were craftsmen who made furniture and everything. They started out by making caskets and other things, and in a lot of towns it was just a combination of a furniture store and a funeral home. A lot of craftsmen were doing that.

I've had a lot of people say, "Funeral directors could write a book," and that's probably true!

Bryson Price, Lewisburg, November 16, 2007

MULTITASKING FUNERAL HOMES

Several years ago, our funeral home here in Hardinsburg operated the funeral service for our county. So, as you can imagine, we were pretty busy conducting funeral services, operating the ambulance service, and running the county coroner's office from our funeral home.

Ann Denton, Hardinsburg, November 9, 2007

VEILED CASKETS

Something you don't see much these days is the use of a veil. In the old days, we always used what we called a veil to spread over the casket, especially if it were a half-couch casket. You'd take the veil and spread it over the open part of the casket.

That practice started out in order to help keep insects, flies, etc., away from the body. That was done especially when bodies were taken to homes. However, we used it now and then, especially when it was needed, and because people were used to it. And we did have different colors. They were pretty and embroidered, and it did help with the color of the deceased.

Every once in a while, you'd have a full-couch casket, but you don't see many of those any more here in this area. In some places you probably could still see them.

William Lee Shannon, Shelbyville, October 25, 2007

REMEMBRANCES IN CASKETS

A lot of kids, especially, will fix notes and stuff to put in the casket when a family member dies. It's a shame that throughout the lives people go through, they don't tell others how much they appreciate them. But at the time of death, I guess people seem to find comfort in writing notes, even though the person is deceased. I guess it helps them mend some fences they should have done years ago. We have a lot of things like that put in the casket. We've also buried money in caskets.

Bryson Price, Lewisburg, November 16, 2007

MEMORY SAFES IN CASKETS

Some caskets now have what are called memory safes, which are little drawers.

If the family wants to put something in there, such as a written letter, there is a little place in which you can put a thank-you note at the bottom of the casket. I always ask family members if they are going to put things in the casket, such as pieces of jewelry.

Rayfield Houghlin, Bloomfield, October 17, 2007

HELPING FATHER

I was born December 11, 1925, and that put me at exactly the right age to get me in World War II, and it got me into the funeral business when things were transferring from the way they used to be to the way it is now. I spent about three years in the navy and got out. The Veterans Administration paid my funeral school tuition and sent me a little money to eat and sleep on.

Funeral customs have changed very much in the past years. Back when I was a growing boy, my dad had a cabinet shop, so he basically home-made the caskets. He had a funeral director's license, which at that time was more about record keeping and death certificates than it is now. So if a death occurred at night, he generally got me up to help him. So, I'd go up and help him make the coffin, as he called it. We made them as needed. He didn't make any ahead of time, for some people had broad shoulders and were narrow-toed. He bought the handles and lining from the National Casket Company. He kept those.

When there was a death, he would generally take me along with him just as a helper. At that time, a death generally occurred at a home, and it was usually necessary to take the bed down and out of the room and then put the casket in there.

I can remember seeing many bedbugs! They inhabited the straw ticks, which were in common use at that time.

Charles McMurtrey, Summer Shade, July 29, 2007

HELPING OTHERS

Dad went to school a little bit to get his funeral director's license, but he could not do embalming. He got Jess Hatcher in Glasgow to do that when needed. My dad had a philosophy that he would treat everybody just the same way; there was no difference because of who they were. If they had money, that was all right. If they didn't, he would wait. He would leave me here at the funeral home in the late forties, early fifties, when there were a lot of stillborn babies.

He would buy a dozen two-foot caskets at the same time. He said that if a woman carried her pregnancy for nine months and the child was stillborn, the family generally did the needed burials. He said they were entitled to the best wishes and services from neighbors and kinfolks. Of course, the doctor signed the document stating that it was a stillborn baby that was being buried.

I'd tell my father that so-and-so came in and needed the casket, and that I sold them one and that they said to tell my father they would pay him. He said, "That's all right. It made you feel good, didn't it?"

I said, "Yeah, they was kind of down and out and I was kindly helping them out, and that made them feel good."

Charles McMurtrey, Summer Shade, July 29, 2007

REMEMBERING WHEN

When I came to work here at the Bosley Funeral Home, all the Bosleys were deceased except Cranston Bosley, and he [had] had a stroke back in the late 1940s. Thus, he was not very active, and then his son died in 1969. I bought the funeral home then.

Cranston Bosley's father was the person that started this funeral home back in 1871. So they go back to horse-and-buggy times and also had the first motorized hearse. Back then, they had funeral visitations at home. Cranston's father was a person like you see in cowboy movies. He was a furniture dealer. He sold furniture in his store, and he also sold caskets there, then delivered them to the homes after the body was embalmed. He would come back later to dress the body and put it in the casket. Then he would come back on the day of the funeral and actually take the horse-drawn hearse to the church, then on to the cemetery for the actual burial. Things were different back then. Times were slower, and more central.

So many attitudes and people's values of life—from inner-city Louisville back in the 1960s to rural life out here in Lebanon now—have changed so very much. Lebanon is a part of rural America. There are a lot more funeral visitations here, as people know a lot more about each other. In Louisville, we might have ten to twenty people come to visit somebody, but here in Lebanon, we might have a couple of hundred visitors, because we live a closer life to each other.

James R. Moraja Sr., Lebanon, March 28, 2008

TRAGEDY IN CEMETERY

Oddly enough, here in our community we had a lady that killed one of her children in a cemetery, or maybe it was two that she killed. I think this happened way back in the 1930s. After she killed her young children, she actually cut her own throat.

She probably had a mental problem. The cemetery caretaker found her, so they were able to save her life. He ran from the cemetery and got help, and the police went back. She wasn't dead. She tried to kill herself by cutting her throat, but she didn't cut her throat deep enough.

She wasn't mentally stable, so she was never penalized. It was just a sad situation. When talking about this one cemetery, people always refer back to the lady that killed her children and tried to kill herself. I've heard that story many, many times.

James R. Moraja Sr., Lebanon, March 28, 2008

EARLY AFRICAN AMERICAN CARE FOR THE DEAD

I'm not old enough, but history has told me that it was a tradition to place coins on the eyes of the deceased. Back then it was the women as well as the men that had certain roles that they played when a death occurred. Women were the "wet nurses"; they were the ones on plantations, or during slavery times, that were in the house taking care of whoever the sick may be. They didn't have doctors that were sometimes available, so it was the responsibility of the slaves to wet the brow of their master, or the children, or the family. So, when they would become ill, it were the slaves that were in there tending to the needs of the individual. Family members standing outside the door would ask, "How is she doing?"

So, when the death occurred, it was the slaves that would remove them from the house and do what needed to be done. It wasn't actually the master and his family saying, "Oh, let's gather up Mom." It was them telling them where to take her and what to do in that process. So that was the caretakers taking care of the ill and the dying and the dead. Thus, it would only be natural for African Americans to be in the funeral industry and make it a profession.

Although the women were the ones that were always taking care of the sick and the dying and the dead, it took a man to decide to make it a profession. [Laughter]

Gayle Graham, Louisville, May 1, 2008

(Some of Gayle Graham's comments were based on an unpublished essay by Erich March, "The History of the African-American Funeral Service: Our 'Home-Going' Heritage." March is vice president of March Funeral Homes in Baltimore, MD.)

Early Practice in Shelbyville

E. M. Coots and Son had a funeral home in Shelbyville from 1830 to 1860. They then moved to Jeffersonville, Indiana. Some of their family is probably still active there.

In early years, the term "funeral home" was not used. Funeral practice was conducted in a place where the funeral equipment was stored. They met people and sold furniture along with being a funeral director. Thus, it is hard to use the term "funeral home" in that situation.

In the old days, even when I came along, we were still doing embalming in the home. Not very much of that is being done these days. My funeral home has not done that in over fifty years. We wouldn't be prepared to go to homes anymore, due to the equipment we use now.

When I first started in the business back in the 1940s, even in the 1950s, we were still doing preparations in the homes. We would go in, take our daybed, and all the equipment we needed to do embalming. We did the work in their parlor, bedroom, or wherever it needed to be done. Quite often the family helped us do different things.

Most of the folks I ran into while doing these things had already experienced what was taking place. Most of the early work was done in homes. What we did was do the embalming, then put the deceased's body back in bed. After that, we took the casket out the next day, or next two days, and placed the body in the casket and took it to be buried. Quite often we took it to the church and had the funeral service there. Or, the service was held at home some of the time.

We were at this location at Eighth and Main Street, here in Shelbyville. The building was a two-story structure with an apartment upstairs, garage in the back. We moved from there to a private home in 1941 located right next door to my personal home now. Our firm was called Shannon Undertaking Company for many years but later on was changed to Shannon Funeral Service.

William Lee Shannon, Shelbyville, October 25, 2007

Black Funeral Home in Shelbyville

We had a black funeral home here in Shelbyville. Daisy Morgan Saffell was one of the first black ladies to be licensed as an embalmer in Kentucky. That happened in 1909; then she died in 1918. After that, it was carried on by Professor Saffell. Of course, at that time they did all the black work.

There is still a black funeral home here. . . . The funeral home is known as Morton-Beckley Funeral Home. They cater to the black community here. Mr. Beckley just recently died, so I don't know what's going to happen. He was a nice gentleman.

The black community [now] uses all three funeral homes, as each family chooses.

William Lee Shannon, Shelbyville, October 25, 2007

FUNERAL DIRECTORS AND EMBALMERS

There is a difference between a funeral director and an embalmer. Just the funeral director is in charge of picking the body up at the place of death and bringing the body in to the funeral home. Then, somebody that is an embalmer would do the embalming. There's no law that says you have to embalm, but if you have an open casket you do have to embalm. Funeral directors can do embalming but need a double license.

The funeral director is involved with picking the body up, making arrangements with the family for the funeral, getting all the details of that together, and being present when the funeral takes place. My kids are just licensed funeral directors, thus have nothing to do with embalming.

Bob Brown, Elizabethtown, September 25, 2007

MORTUARY SCHOOL

You have to have schooling in order to get an embalmer's license. But just to be a funeral director, you don't have to go to mortuary school. In some cases, wives of funeral directors have just gotten their funeral director's license. Instead of going to school, they've just obtained only one license.

The mortuary school I attended was in Jeffersonville, Indiana. It was called Mid-America College of Funeral Service. The old school used to be in Louisville, and they had a school in Indianapolis. Several years ago, they combined those two schools, and put it in Jeffersonville. Before they merged, the school in Louisville was known as the Kentucky School of Embalming. I'm not sure about the one in Indiana, but I think it was either the Indianapolis or Indiana School of Embalming. That was in the early 1980s, and I was in one of the first classes that actually graduated from the Mid-America College.

I am both a funeral director and an embalmer, and I graduated from the Mortuary College in 1983. I've been licensed for several years now, and I intend to keep working like this until I'm gone!

Bryson Price, Lewisburg, November 16, 2007

EMBALMING AT HOME

When my grandfather started Hughes Funeral Service, they ran an ambulance service along with the funeral business, and those stories we'll have to keep for another time. In those days the mortician would come to the home of the deceased and do the embalming there.

The corpse would lay in state at the home until after the funeral, [and then] the body was taken to the graveyard for interment. Grandfather took his instruments to the home in somewhat of a doctor's bag. He used a hand pump to inject the embalming fluid. That was before the days of electricity and indoor plumbing.

My grandmother assisted him by doing the pumping. When that was finished, it was pumped into a bucket. And my father says he can remember having to dig a hole about two feet deep by using posthole diggers. The body fluids were then deposited in the hole.

Connie Hughes Goodman, Fountain Run, September 11, 2007

EARLY EMBALMING METHODOLOGY

Mr. Will Alvey at the Perry and Alvey Funeral Home here in Elizabethtown is an older gentleman and a great guy, a very smart man. He was raised up in that business. Mr. A. F. Dyer, the originator of that funeral home, was Mr. Alvey's father-in-law. He used to tell stories about having a death call in the days before telephones and almost before cars. People would have to come in to the funeral home to get service, or they'd have to send word somehow. Of course, they never did bring bodies in. So the funeral homes would have to load up their stuff and go out into the country and do the embalming right there in the home. And since the roads weren't any good, the funeral directors would have to spend the night. It might take them all day just to get to the other end of the county. They'd spend the night, and they might just stay there until time for the funeral service and then have the burial.

I've heard Will Alvey tell many stories like that. Of course, that would be pretty rough today. Back then they had what was called a cooling board that they carried into the house, put the body on it, and did the embalming. They'd do that right on the bed where the person died. Of course, back then everybody died at home and the embalming was done right there. Back then they had an embalming instrument that pushed and pulled at the same time. I remember seeing one once. We have machines to do it now, but they used to do it by hand.

Bob Brown, Elizabethtown, September 25, 2007

EMBALMING HISTORY

Of course, the primary purpose of embalming, even to this day, is for disinfection. That's why embalming came into being. In the 1800s, people were catching all kinds of communicable diseases, because when we die the microorganisms—the anaerobic organisms, which multiply by the millions without oxygen—will grow and will cause all kinds of disease.

The primary purpose of embalming has always been, and still is to this day, the disinfection of the body so these organisms won't grow. Of course, [with] the pharaohs and the Egyptians, some of the things that are unearthed even today and have been unearthed in previous years, people would not want us to embalm that way. The way they embalmed back then was cutting the body open, getting rid of the organs, and dipping the body in salts and resins for seventy days; they laid them out on a board in the hot, dry sun for seventy days.

What happened was, there was no bacteria left. They had killed all the bacteria by natural progression. So therefore they had no decomposition, and they would wrap them in fine linen cloths as mummies, if you please. Thus, there was no decomposition after that. And a lot of people don't realize that's the way this was done, so that's why you have the mummification of hundreds and hundreds of years ago.

Terry Dabney, Campbellsville, October 13, 2007

TAYLOR COUNTY'S FIRST FUNERAL HOME

The first funeral home in this area was probably founded by John Robert McFarland in 1921 in Willowtown. The Parrott and Ramsey Funeral Home here in Campbellsville is a direct descendant of that funeral home. There's a picture I have of a horse-drawn hearse that says "Parrott and Ramsey since 1923." It was taken in 1948 at the Centennial Parade in

Campbellsville and was a photo of Mr. McFarland's horse-drawn carriage and his horses. Johnny Maupin was the driver, and I know all the other people involved.

Before McFarland's funeral home was established, burials around here took place by just neighbors and friends coming in. Furniture makers built the caskets that were used. Actually, most people called them coffins back then, and some people still call them coffins. Probably the term "casket" came into vogue in the mid-1930s. Prior to the mid-1930s, many people made their own wooden coffins.

Terry Dabney, Campbellsville, October 13, 2007

LAST EMBALMING IN THE HOLLER

The next story I want to share is about the last embalming in the holler. It was about 1969 when this family came in and said, "Uncle Bill died up in the holler, and Uncle Bill has not been out of that holler in about twenty-five years." They wanted to know if we could go up there and embalm him and take care of everything without having to take him out of the holler.

The funeral home I worked at was one of these places where if it could be done, they'd do it, as long as it was legal. So they decided that they would go down in the basement and get out the old house equipment they had.

In the basement we got the cooling board, which is what was called an embalming table they took to the house. We had a gravity machine, which is fed by gravity. The higher up you hang it, the more per-pound pressure you have to inject into bodies. We had the gravity machine, and we had the old hand pump to do the aspirating with. Everything seemed to be working all right. Bige Hoskins was the embalmer. He and an assistant headed up to the holler. They got up there, and of course, the family didn't know just exactly what to expect. Quite frankly, neither did Bige or his assistant, because they had never embalmed anybody at home before.

So they took some rubber sheets, spread them out, set up the old cooling board, which kind of looks like a little table that folds in half. It's about four foot when you fold it and about eight foot long when it is unfolded. They placed Uncle Bill on the table, then started gathering up buckets and things to put the body fluids in. Bige was trying to figure how it was going to be proper, etc., with everybody there, because they all wanted to stay there and make sure Uncle Bill was taken care of.

Bige proceeded to undress Uncle Bill, but the family didn't know all that stuff that had to be done, so Bige explained to them, "We need to bathe Uncle Bill, clean him up, and straighten him up to give him a nice appearance."

Well, Uncle Bill's family decided they would just do that. They undressed Uncle Bill and bathed him the best they could, while Bige was watching. Once they got that done, they said, "Now, Mr. Hoskins, you just go ahead and do whatever you need to do."

So, Bige went ahead with the embalming, setting the features, the arms, and the hands. Of course, by this time rigor mortis had set in a little bit, so that made it a little harder working around on Uncle Bill. Bige was getting ready to inject the body.

They had a unique circumstance. They had a gravity bottle but nothing to hang it by. Bige explained to them what he needed, so they went out and got an eye hook and came back and took a hand drill and drilled a hole in the ceiling and screwed in the eye hook. So, Bige got his gravity bottle working, and he proceeded to inject one gallon at a time. Everything went real well, and they didn't know what to do with the by-product of the embalming fluid, which was the blood and stuff taken from the body, so they decided to pour it in the outhouse. Bige found out about that and wasn't real happy about it because he had told them to bury it. So he asked if they had any lime around there anywhere. Of course, being on a farm up in the head of the holler, they've got lime. So they poured it in the outhouse to kind of neutralize the body fluids and stuff.

Bige asked them if they wanted to step out of the room while he did the aspirating, because that's kind of hard on some folks who are not aware of what that is. They all decided that they might want to step out of the room. It wasn't the easiest thing to do, but Bige went ahead and tried to aspirate by using the hand pump, especially a hand pump that was one hundred years old.

Once they got done with that, Bige put the cavity fluid in and decided to leave the button out in case the gas built up. So he then asked them about clothing. Well, they decided that since they had cleaned Uncle Bill, the least they could do was to dress him.

The men came in there and dressed Uncle Bill in a brand-new flannel shirt, long red flannel underwear, bib overalls, and a new pair of boots. Caps weren't quite in style like they are today, so a lot of the old boys had old felt hats they used to wear back in the thirties, forties, and early fifties. Uncle Bill had one of them hats he just really liked, so they put it on him.

Then it came time for the casket. Bige said, "Well, you all need to go back by the funeral home to pick out a casket."

They said, "No, Uncle Bill made his own casket."

Bige was kind of intrigued by that, as not many people still made their own caskets back then. But sure enough, they went out to the barn, and up in the loft was Uncle Bill's casket. But it had been made for quite a while, and the interior had got a little dry-rotted. So when they got it out, Bige said, "Well we need to do something about this interior."

Well, a couple of ladies had some homemade quilts. Quilting back then was quite an everyday thing, and everybody had homemade quilts. So, they took out the old lining from the casket. Then the ladies took some tacks and things and put a quilt lining in Uncle Bill's casket. Bige put Uncle Bill in his casket and proceeded to have visitation there at the house.

We took our house equipment, which consisted of a house drape, a register stand, hand fans, and things like that. They didn't have any electricity up in the holler, so they used coal oil lamps. Everything worked out just fine. Visitation went on for two days. On the third day, they had the funeral service there on the front porch of the house. That was kind of an old-time tradition, if the weather was nice and pretty. Back at that time, it was still a fairly common thing to have everything at home.

Anyway, they had the funeral there, and Uncle Bill and his casket there on the front porch. Everything went well. Then they took Uncle Bill up to the cemetery.

Back then, most of the time, friends dug the grave. They dug Uncle Bill what they called "digging a vault." What that means is that you go down about three and one-half foot; then you come in about six or eight inches, depending on how wide the grave is. Then you go down about another two and one-half foot. The reason for this is that they would lower Uncle Bill's homemade casket down into the vault. Then they'd place a row of boards, usually cedar or yellow poplar, something that would kind of hold up underground, and then come back with another layer of boards over the tops of the cracks. That would keep the dirt and stuff off of Uncle Bill and the weight of the earth off his casket. They filled in the grave, then proceeded to have a little committal.

Bige came back to the funeral home and told Billy Engle, "Now, I want you to know, this is the last embalming that we're doing outside the funeral home. We're not embalming out in the houses anymore. This is it; we're done."

To my knowledge, that was the last home embalming in the mountains, and that was in the late 1960s.

Jay Steele, Pineville, January 20, 2008

Coming of the Electronic Age

I have noticed the funeral profession changing insofar as the way family members eulogize their loved ones. . . . With the electronic age, we now use a lot more DVDs, CDs, etc., to assist a family in eulogizing their loved ones. And today, families are having less religious-type services and are having family members do more eulogies at their level.

William Fields, Ashland, May 7, 2008

Early Years versus Present Times

Back then, in early days, we would go out and make a removal of the body. Then the family would come in to the funeral home and make a selection. Then we would prepare the body, and just as soon as we could get it loaded and ready, we'd load up all the equipment, and even if it was four o'clock in the morning, take the artificial setup for the body to be placed in at the residence. Then we'd get the door badges, the chairs, and everything that it took, such as artificial drapes, lamps. Then we'd take the body back to the residence to remain there until time for the services, which sometimes would be held in the residence. Sometimes we'd go to a church.

After a period of time, that became a little more inconvenient, so people started letting us bring the bodies in to the funeral home to embalm. Then they would come in and we would stay at the funeral home, but then go to churches for all funerals.

As time began to progress down through the years, funeral chapels were being built to take the place of the churches. So we had the chapels built onto the funeral homes, and we started using the chapels instead of going to the churches for the funerals.

Today, about 99 percent of our funerals are conducted in the chapels rather than going to the church. That started taking place around 1958. We started seeing changes at that time, then on, until the early 1960s.

Charles Strode, Tompkinsville, May 29, 2008

LOTS OF CHANGES

A lot of the changes in the funeral profession have to do with the preparation of the body that was once done primarily in the home. Then it moved from that to the funeral home, from which the bodies would then be taken back to the home for visitation, kept out a couple of days, and then taken to the church for funeral services.

It began to change in the 1960s when bodies were left at the funeral home. Then the chapels were built, and they started using funeral homes for funeral services. It has been a vast change across the years. Cremation has crept into our society at a tremendous rate that I never thought I would see. In some funeral homes, they have a business rate of cremations up to about 28 percent. However, in our area, it is still not hardly that strong. But I really see that the trend has been that people don't have time to get off from work, or they don't want to take time, so they feel like cremation is the easy way out and the less expensive way out. So, they just ask for direct cremation. Then they can get on with their lives.

A rental casket came along that was made available, and some families want to use that at this point in time in order to have a traditional service. However, they don't want the in-ground burial, so therefore they just use a rental casket to do a memorial service. Then they will place the cremated remains at a later date in a cemetery they prefer.

There's been a tremendous change in casket manufacturing, vaults, and this type of stuff, compared to what it used to be. Let's say that in 1956 they primarily had three colors of caskets—copper, gray, and white. That was usually all funeral homes had to offer. An expensive casket would have a full bed, or what we call "an expensive couch casket." Then that kind of went by the wayside, and people started using half-couch caskets. Color schemes also became a big factor, as everybody wanted different colors. Thus, manufactures got into it by coming up with a lot of colors for caskets. Today, we have a various number of color schemes we have to deal with so families can make selections of merchandise.

Hardwood caskets were very prevalent at one time, but they went out of existence when metal, copper, and bronze went into existence. But we see a trend these days of people going back to using the hard-wood caskets, even though hardwood caskets these days are made out of poplar, oak, hickory, cherry, walnut, cedar, and pecan. A lot of it is very elaborate, almost as if it is an elaborate piece of furniture now, due to the way caskets are made and the high quality of detailed work that goes in them.

So over a period of years, it was from wood to metal, and then from metal to wood. Times have changed, and people don't have much time anymore to do anything but bury the dead.

Charles Strode, Tompkinsville, May 29, 2008

PROFESSIONAL PRIDE

In the funeral business, I think it is vital that you have a sense of humor because of the things you deal with on a daily basis for those families that you serve. Funeral directors are serving people at the lowest point in their lives. They don't want to see you in the first place, and things that shouldn't bother them tear them all to pieces, while things that should bother them buzz right by.

I am proud of my profession. For those of us who stay in it and dedicate ourselves to serving our families, there is nothing more reward-ing than when a wife comes up and you've just buried her husband and she says, "You don't know how much I appreciate what you have done to help me." Or, when children come up and have lost both of their parents in a tragic accident and say, "You know, I don't know what we would have done if it hadn't been for you all."

I actually grew up around funeral directors. My dad was a funeral director, and he served his apprenticeship in the Engle Funeral Home in the 1940s, and I served mine there in the 1970s. I worked there from 1965 to 1993. I've been very fortunate to have worked with a lot of good funeral directors. There were Bige Hoskins, Billy Engle, and Casey Compton. One of the funeral directors I worked with was Rus-sell Compton, who was just a fantastic person with families. I learned things about professionalism, about giving and caring. There is no more rewarding service in the funeral service than helping families in their greatest need. I am proud to say that I am a funeral director, and I am proud to share the humorous stories that we have here, but there are so many sad stories that any funeral director could share with you.

Things such as family tragedies, mass disasters, automobile accidents, and suicides are some of the things we come into contact with.

There is a high turnover in the funeral profession because, quite frankly, it is a very tough business to be in. You have to be able to shoulder the responsibilities and harness the mental stress that you deal with, because if you can't serve the families there, then you are not helping anybody. And they call on you to guide them through the worst hours of their lives.

In the end, when they come up to you and give you a hug and call your name and say, "You just don't know how much you have helped us get through this, and I sure do thank you." That right there sums up why I like being a funeral director. I'm not in it for the money because you're sure not going to get rich, but it sure is nice when somebody comes up and says, "I appreciate what you have done to help me." And that makes me proud to be a funeral director.

I'm also proud of the fact that I got in it back when some of the old-time fellows were there, like Bige Hoskins, Russell Compton, Shorty Bullock, Bob Walden, Jim Buchanan, my father, Julius M. Steele, and people like them—just any number of funeral directors that I'm proud to say that I've learned something from, that they helped mould me and showed me the right way to do things in this profession.

Jay Steele, Pineville, March 1, 2008

BEST JOB IN THE WORLD

Being a funeral director has been a good job. It's a job that if you like it, it's the best job in the world, and if you don't like it, it's the worst job in the world.

Rayfield Houghlin, Bloomfield, October 17, 2007

2

Funeral and Burial Folk Customs

~

A folk custom is a way of behaving in accordance with family and community traditions from the "old times," the good old days people often view as ideal. Folk customs are passed on from one generation to the next, and they are usually kept in place by expectations of compliance and by disapproval of violations.

In early times, it was common for families to prepare for the death of a loved one. It was also common for family and gracious community members to dress dead persons' bodies, to dig graves, and to provide homegrown flowers for grave sites and Memorial Day services. People often built their own caskets, usually called coffins, and made their own burial clothing. Amish and Mennonite communities still respect and utilize the traditional ways of preparing for and conducting burials, and the same is true for other communities in some remote sections of the Commonwealth.

On occasion, despite preparation and tradition, the unexpected occurred, such as movements of a body. Sometimes funeral and burial folk customs included handling of serpents, dramatic faintings, and other "rites of passage." But more often, funeral services and burials followed a predictable pattern.

Chairs were typically provided at the grave site for bereaved family members and friends. Those without chairs stood in a circle surrounding the grave. A passage was read from the Bible and the minister provided a brief devotional. After that, the casket was lowered into the grave. Family members usually remained at the grave site even after the burial was completed in order to be the first to place a floral tribute on the newly mounded grave. There they began the process of returning to their regular way of living. Southern funerals were sad events, but they also emphasized that social existence is perpetual and enduring and helps preserve the traditional way of life.

DIGGING GRAVES WAS COMMUNITY RESPONSIBILITY

I remember when digging graves was the responsibility of the neighborhood. They dug them and they filled them up. Digging of a grave was kind of a community gathering. That's where they did most of their talking about the dead person. And these community people would remain there to watch as the casket was being covered over with soil and the grave was being filled up.

The word "coffin" is still used occasionally, but "casket" is the word that is normally used in present times.

Charles McMurtrey, Summer Shade, July 29, 2007

OLD-TIME BURIAL CUSTOMS

It's still possible that you can bury a member of your own family, but you can't go out and bury a person in somebody else's family. Legally, you can bury your own if you want to. A death certificate has to be filled out and signed by a funeral director. Amish families in and around Sonora, here in Hardin County, don't use a funeral home. We've made out death certificates for them, and they just bury the dead. They don't embalm. They make their own caskets, and they have their own services, during which they take the body out to the cemetery and bury it. That still happens.

Once in a while, somebody will be buried on their own property, like people did many years ago. However, in most cases nowadays funeral homes are involved.

I've got a great-grandfather and great-grandmother that are buried at Dead Horse Hollow, located in Meade County. They're out in a field with cattle. The cemetery is called Brown Family Cemetery, and it is a mess.

I know about where it is located, but I've never been there. I'm afraid of those copperhead snakes down there!

Bob Brown, Elizabethtown, September 25, 2007

HOMEGROWN FLOWERS

Flowers for graves used to be homegrown, or perhaps made out of crepe paper. However, during spring and summer, flowers were homegrown.

And people often made them during the summer to be used later on when needed for funerals or for placing on graves on Memorial Day.

Charles McMurtrey, Summer Shade, July 29, 2007

CLOSED MOUTH

We've gone to homes to pick up bodies, and some local person had actually taken pieces of cloth, cut them, and tied the cloth around the dead person's chin and the top of their head in order to close their mouth. That's happened a few times, and it was done by local people.

Bryson Price, Lewisburg, November 16, 2007

CLOSED EYES

Back then friends and neighbors did the biggest part of the work involved in a funeral. Men would shave the face of a dead neighbor man, and women would fix the hair of a dead woman and dress them. It was a custom back then to put a coin on each eye of the deceased. That practice stopped after embalming came into vogue and got accepted by local people. When embalmed, if the eye was dry, people shifted from quarters because you could close the eye and the eye would stay closed.

Charles McMurtrey, Summer Shade, July 29, 2007

PREACHER MADE HIS OWN CASKET

I know of a person who made his own casket. He made it out of wood, and in terms [of] height, he made it, like, one foot by twelve or one by fourteen. Of course, he didn't make it deep enough like caskets are today. And he had a flat top on it, and the casket was tall enough to accommodate him, but for handles he put stair rails on the side. But they stuck out so far that when they took him to church his casket wouldn't go through the door. However, they didn't know about it until they got to church, so they had to take the handles off the casket in order to go into the church. When they opened the casket, they had to lift him up to make him more viewable, because he was laying flat on the bottom of the casket.

That man designed his own casket, and that's the way it had to work. Oddly enough, he was a minister, and he had thought for several years about building his casket. So he built it and stored it until he actually used it. His casket was quite different than what you would think of today. It was a wooden box, basically too thick, and designed like you see on old Western movies—narrow at the bottom and wider at the top.

We didn't have his funeral, but I went to his funeral. He died— probably back in the 1970s.

James R. Moraja Sr., Lebanon, March 28, 2008

LONG-WINDED PREACHERS

For a funeral service, we went on to the church with the body and always had four or five preachers to take part in the service. Well, one wasn't about to let the others get ahead of him. If one spoke twenty minutes, the other one was going to speak twenty-five minutes, and a little louder!

After the preachers were finished, in earlier times the people would sit right there at the graveside and watch you shovel every inch of dirt on top of the body before they would leave. Nowadays people want to leave, so we won't put any dirt on the casket until after the family leaves and we lower the body into the grave. One of us funeral directors always stays and helps lower the casket to see to it that it's proper before we leave.

That's going back a long time—almost forty years.

Terry Dabney, Campbellsville, October 13, 2007

PREACHER COMPETITION

Traditionally, some of the United Baptists and Old Regular Baptists in this area take half a day to preach a funeral. They do that more-so in their churches than they do here at the funeral home. During a funeral, we usually have a tag team of preachers, anywhere from two to five, something like that. It appears that each one of them tries to outdo the others as to how long they take during the service.

William Fields, Ashland, May 7, 2008

AFRICAN AMERICAN WAKES AND VISITATIONS

Times do change. We used to talk about coffins, but now we call them caskets. In earlier times we talked about "wakes," and now we talk about "visitations." They are one and the same. It's actually the time that is allotted for people in the public to be able to come into the funeral home and express their sympathy to the family and pay respects to the deceased and share, hopefully, some positive stories or say something memorable to the family. We find that those people that work on a job and probably put in at least forty hours per week are kindly like a work family. Then, there are the actual biological children and parents, and then you may be involved in some social or civic things that make up your social and civic family. It's amazing how one person can be involved in so many things, but they are the unifying entity in that group

When you have a "wake" in the African American black culture, our wakes may not be quiet, because they are also family reunions, or home-goings. We find that people will come and get so excited when they see a person that they haven't seen for ten or twelve years. It's not that they're not celebrating the life of the deceased individual; it's like, "I haven't seen you in ten years!" So what it is, they're having a homecoming.

So, the purpose of the wake was to stay up with the body all night and protect the body from all the myths and superstitions that went with that. For example, in case the person wasn't really dead, you wanted to be there to help them if by some chance they were not completely gone. It is said that some people used to do that, but I assure anyone that if the embalming process has taken place, there is NO accidental waking up. If we've done our job right, that is not the issue! [Laughter]

Actually, the term "wake" is still used by some black people and some white people. It is probably an age word as opposed to an ethnic word. Those persons of a certain age would probably say, "When is the wake?" Then someone else may say, "What is a wake?"

I think they changed the term "wake" to "visitation" to say it is visiting with the family or the loved one. But the term "wake" is still used, just like coffin and casket.

Gayle Graham, Louisville, May 1, 2008

SERVICES FOR THE AMISH AND MENNONITES

The Amish normally call the funeral home here in order to have the body properly embalmed. When that is completed, they'll say, "If it's okay, we'll take care of it."

They do that ahead of time. They call to get in contact with me prior to any deaths. They want to do it legally, right, and the way it should be. That's the reason they contact me. I've done this a couple of times. We'll do the embalming, then take the body on a cot to the house or wherever they say.

They build their own caskets, make their own clothing for the body, dress the body, lay the body out, have their own funeral. Sometimes there are hundreds of people at the funeral. I've been to these funerals. They are very dignified and very nice.

That still happens. The Amish and the Mennonites would be the same to me in the way I handle things, but it would not be to them. I just want to say that they do it very respectfully and very good. They are good people, very honest and forthright in letting us know what's going on, and wanting us to do programs, etc., for them. So, anything they want, we do, and anything they don't want, we don't do. Thus, our main service to them is filling out the formal death certificates.

Terry Dabney, Campbellsville, October 13, 2007

LEGAL REQUIREMENTS

People used to bury their own family members and community members. That was done for many, many years in the old days. Throughout Shelby County, there are many family cemeteries. Several years ago, the historical society made a great detailed survey and published a book on these cemeteries. A KET-television description about home funerals is currently being shown.

A lot of things are still being done, and you don't have to have embalming done. It is not a law requirement. And you can take care of your own family if you get permission to bury them, but to do so you have to do some paperwork. State laws in the United States are different along these lines. In Kentucky, you must file a death certificate and secure a burial transit permit.

William Lee Shannon, Shelbyville, October 25, 2007

DECEASED WAS A WOODS COLT

Some words and expressions last for a few years, or even a decade or two, while others hang on forever it seems. There are situations when people use words that go back through several generations, and the people who hear these words later are in the dark.

This particular story happened over in Edmonson County at Jerry Patton's funeral home. This lady funeral director was waiting on a family by making arrangements, gathering information for the funeral, and filling out the death certificate, when she came to a question no one was answering.

It was and is our custom to first ask for information about the mother of the deceased, because that gives you a clue as to whether the father is known or not, so you can smoothly get over this hurdle early in the process. Usually someone will say, "Born out of wedlock," or, "She went by her mother's last name."

But this time, no one spoke up. Finally someone said quietly, "She was a woods colt." So the lady started writing and spelling out loud as she wrote *w-o-o-d-s*. Then she realized what was being said, even though she had not heard that word before. She just skipped to the next question, never looking up, and never stopped asking the questions.

The family was using "woods colt," an old word that was once used to denote illegitimate birth, because they didn't want to say illegitimate. That lady never forgot that word.

James M. Pendley, Morgantown, March 3, 2008

POTENTIAL THIEVERY

They used to have to undress and dress the person's body. And most of the time they dropped the worn clothes out the window because they *needed* to go out the window. That was the procedure, but on one occasion a family got upset because they thought somebody had stole his money.

That happened over at Sulphur Lick. It could have happened because when they handed those overalls out the window back then, whoever got them would have felt in the pocket.

Charles McMurtrey, Summer Shade, July 29, 2007

Dressing the Deceased

This is a story about how community members would help with funerals years ago. On Sand Hill, which is located out of Livingston a piece, they had this man named Boney Mink that died. They called another man there in the community to come in and lay him out. His name was Ellis Marshall. He said he'd never helped like that before.

I think it might have been cool weather, but he was in there trying to get this dead man cleaned up and get burial clothes on him. Marshall said that he wrestled him around but couldn't get his clothes on. But finally, since rigor mortis had already set in, and the dead man was stiff as a poker, he stood him up in a corner of the room and got his clothes on.

The fellow was tall and skinny and didn't weigh anything hardly, so Marshall stood him up there in the corner and finally got him dressed and got him put in a casket. Back then, somebody came in and dug the grave, and they laid them out at home.

Billy Dowell, Mt. Vernon, August 27, 2007

Making Wooden Funeral Boxes

This happened at the Red Hill section of the county. We had someone there at the funeral home laid out. John D. Shepherd from Red Hill was there the night before, and whoever it was that we had, they was going to be buried in a wood box instead of the vault. John D. said, "Dowell, boy, them old pond [pine] boxes ain't too much account, are they? Would it be all right if I made them a good ole oak box?"

He had a sawmill. I said, "Why sure."

He said, "Well, give me the dimensions, and I'll have it at the cemetery tomorrow."

I wrote down how big to make that box, and the funeral was going on the next day when the phone rang. It was John D., and he said "Dowell, boy, I made the first mistake I ever made in my life. I made that damn box too little." [Laughter]

I'm sure he hadn't even made the first lick on it. Well, we had to run around there and find a box and get it to the cemetery.

Billy Dowell, Mt. Vernon, August 27, 2007

UNUSUAL ITEMS IN CASKETS

Items are sometimes placed in a casket by a family member. I've had marijuana put in the casket [and] whiskey, money, the dead person's knife, coins, beer, the Bible. Putting the Bible in the casket is really common, but the whiskey and marijuana are not that common. Some of these things do happen, even now.

Family members choose the appropriate items to be placed in the casket because they are what the dead persons liked while they were living.

There was one instance in which we put two or three dollars in a money clip, then put it in their pocket. His widow said that he never did like to be without a few dollars in his pocket. So she sent him to his grave with that money in his pocket.

And we have buried people with diamonds, which I thought was a waste.

Billy Dowell, Mt. Vernon, August 27, 2007

MOURNFUL PRETENDERS

Sometimes we've had people look at the body in the casket, then faint. And sometimes we've had "faints" when it actually wouldn't be a faint. They were just pretending to faint.

For years we've kept a little bottle of something that was commonly used by funeral directors to put under people's nose. It was something like an eggshell that we'd stick under their nose. That was done to keep people from fainting. It was a smelling [salt], and every funeral director carried one in their pocket. They'd reach into their pocket and get out a bottle, or something you could bust like an eggshell, pour it on a piece of cotton, and stick it under their nose. Sometimes they even put it on a toothpick, then stick that into their nose. But if they'd really not fainted, they'd want you to get that smell away from them.

Most of the time, these people weren't fainting, just pretending. And you don't see that now. I haven't seen that for ten years.

I have heard that in some parts of the country a funeral director would hire mourners to mourn at the funeral. He'd holler at the mourners to begin mourning and crying. I've heard of that but never did see it being done.

Edward Dermitt, Leitchfield, August 29, 2007

The Way Burials Used to Be

In the nineteenth century and early years of the twentieth, people had many customs, traditions, and superstitions about burying their dead. Some would stop their clocks, while others hung black cloth over the mirrors in their houses. When someone died suddenly, before a coffin could be built, they would take an interior door off the hinges and lay it across two chairs to place the body on. It is a superstition that a grave must be six foot deep, but that is not true.

On one occasion, our funeral home had to disinter a body. We found it odd to have found a ball of hair at the dead woman's feet. But it was a custom of some to take the hair from the dead person's hairbrush and place it there.

My great-grandmother had to be relocated, and upon digging her up they found that her coffin had a glass lid in it, and they cracked it upon the process of disinterring her. When a person dies, many times their eyes will remain open. Thus, they would place coins upon their eyes to keep their eyes closed.

In earlier years, caskets were traditionally made as a pine box, but later it became fashionable to have a doeskin casket. These caskets had a flat top on them and the handles came separated. My grandfather had to assemble them and put them on the casket. They were shipped in a crate, and sometimes these crates were used as the outside container.

The traditional casket for today is one that the lid opens in two sections, but in the early to mid-1900s, most opened with one solid lid, or one that had two sections that lifted up and sidepieces that folded outward.

Connie Hughes Goodman, Fountain Run, September 11, 2007

More Casket Items

Many strange things have been buried with people's bodies. Some people placed money in the casket with the deceased; some left expensive jewelry on the body of their loved one; and many placed pictures of family members in the casket to be buried with the body. But I guess the oddest thing that was ever placed in a casket with someone was a pint of whiskey. Although there was this one time that we had a body, and my mother said she passed the coffin and the family had placed a cap on the man's chest. The next time she walked by, someone had placed tobacco in his shirt pocket. Then, finally, on the day of the funeral, when she passed by there was an aluminum can in the man's hands. Mother said, "Well, it's whatever the family wants," and that's the way it is. Whatever the family members wish, the funeral directors need to comply if the request is in the capabilities of that particular funeral home.

There was a funeral in Bowling Green in which the deceased relative's pet was put to sleep and placed in the casket with him.

Connie Hughes Goodman, Fountain Run, September 11, 2007

FLOWERS AND MORE

Have you ever wondered why people send flowers to the funeral home? You may say, "Because it shows respect." Or you may say, "It's tradition." Well, you are partially right, as this has become the normal, traditional thing to do. Sending flowers was started many years ago. It actually was started to cover the smell of the decomposing body. I have handled so many flowers in my life that I should smell like a rose!

My dad tells of a time that the flower car was completely full of flowers. He had hired a man by the name of Levy Slaughter to help. When the car became full, Dad asked him, "Now, what are we going to do?"

Levy took his foot, pressed it up against the base of flowers, and gave it a shove. "Bring 'em on," he said.

Many people use the traditional blanket of flowers, but I like to encourage people to make it more personal. In one instance, we placed a quilt on the coffin of the dead lady, who had pieced the quilt herself. In another case, I tried to encourage the family of a man that loved his mules to place a harness on his casket. His family thought it was a lovely idea but didn't have time to clean one up. They also wished that they had had time to hook up the mules to the wagon and haul him to the cemetery in it.

Connie Hughes Goodman, Fountain Run, September 11, 2007

COMMUNITY TRADITIONS

Emotions are strange. I don't think you see as much of it today as you did twenty-five or thirty years ago and farther back—the emotions of how people perceived death and how they countenanced themselves with it. The old traditions and beliefs indicated not only emotions but how they were supposed to show their emotions. You had the emotion, but you also had the dramatics. And there's probably a psychological phenomenon there which I don't fully understand. For example, back then a widow was supposed to wear black for six months. That was a tradition in certain parts of the country, but I don't know how widespread it was, that a lady or widow was to mourn, and also she wasn't to appear in public very much. She would basically wear black or undecorated-type clothing.

I think it came from those traditions, but not only was there the true emotion as to how they expressed their grief, but they also expressed their grief with the dramatics as to how you were supposed to express those emotions. We don't see that anymore.

Not only have we transformed from those traditions in this day and time, but the whole society has transformed from what it was like fifty or so years ago. . . . I'm afraid that we have learned how to socially react—maybe in combination with dramatic programming and the media as a whole—to news and everything else from California and New York and other places rather than to our old traditions of what we thought in communities. I think that's why the community is dissolving. The glue that used to keep a community together is not there anymore.

William Bledsoe, Irvine, September 26, 2007

WORMS AND MORE

A lot of things are placed in the casket of the dead person and buried with them. I've buried a lot of guns. We had this one man who had all these old shotguns and rifles, and he said he didn't want to leave them with anybody in his family, so he said, "I'll just take them with me." So we put these several old guns in the bottom of the casket and buried them with him.

We had somebody else one time that wanted to be buried with their rods and reels. He was a fisherman. Well, we put some of his rods and reels in the casket, and people could actually see these things. The day of the funeral, they came in with a sack and asked me, "Can you put this in the casket, too?"

I said, "Yeah, what's in it?"

They said, "Worms, worms." [Laughter]

I said, "Well, I'll put them in there, but I'm going to seal the sack up so they can't get out."

I guess they wanted the worms in there because they had the rods and reels in there and wanted to provide some bait—just something to catch those fish!

I'll never forget that.

Bob Brown, Elizabethtown, September 25, 2007

Jewelry and More

Right now it's kind of risky to put a lot of jewelry on the body in a chapel. There's nobody in there, and somebody could come in and take it off. I don't know anybody in particular, but I know some funeral homes in bigger cities that have closed circuits, and they watch for things such as that in their office.

I don't recommend that people bring in a lot of fancy things. In fact, if they do, I'd rather they take it home at night. If they want it back on, then bring it back the next morning. I don't like to be held responsible for that.

On one occasion, I was supposed to leave the jewelry on and bury the body with it on, but I took it off. And before the day was over, they said, "Where's the jewelry? Why did you take it off?"

I said, "Well, I don't know. It's a misunderstanding."

They said, "We want it back on."

I said, "Okay," so we had to go back that very day, disinter the body, and put the jewelry back on. That was done at our expense.

On another occasion, about a year ago, I was supposed to take off a watch and a ring on this lady we buried in Meade County. But I forgot to do it. I got a permit from the County Health Department, and we had to go back down there where she was buried. She wasn't in a vault; she was in a casket. We went in there, opened the casket, took off the watch and ring.

I thought it was going to be expensive jewelry, but it wasn't. There was nothing expensive about it. Somebody just wanted it because it belonged to the dead lady.

So, we took it off at our expense!

Bob Brown, Elizabethtown, September 25, 2007

AT-HOME CUSTOMS

There's been many instances when people would make their own casket before they died. They used it as a chest, just like a cedar chest placed at the foot of the bed. They stored blankets and everything else in them. That's happened many, many times, and there wasn't anything thought about it. It was just the way they did things.

Many times, people would more or less conduct their own funeral. In other words, they had their own casket made. In my lifetime, they've always had a funeral director to call, although they didn't bring the body to the funeral home a lot of times. They would embalm the body right at home with the help of neighbors and then set up with the body day and night until they had the funeral. Sometimes they had the funeral at home and sometimes at church.

Terry Dabney, Campbellsville, October 13, 2007

PREPARING THE BODY AT HOME

Back in earlier times people would prepare the body at home to get it ready to be buried. At times, they laid coins on top of each eye in order to weigh down the eyes a little bit. That helped to close the eyes. Coins were about the size of what the eyeballs were. Coins were used for years and years to do that.

As far as dressing the bodies, it was not uncommon for families to go ahead and come in and dress the body for the funeral. We still have that occasionally. Members of the Church of Jesus Christ of Latter Day Saints still come into the homes and dress the bodies of their people. Actually, some other religions still practice that some.

We also have a lot of Amish that have moved into our area now, and the only two Amish burial services we have had since they moved here were two babies. They have come in to talk to us, and the way they do things is to contact us at the time of a death, like it was for these two babies. When they contacted us, we went and picked up the body to embalm it, then took it unclothed back to the home.

I recall that when the babies died, the grandmothers came in and helped the mothers dress the little babies. And they had a workshop right outside the homes, and it was there that they dressed the body and had the visitation, and all other things—there in the little workshop.

We went out there and checked on them every day, but they had visitation for three to four days before they ended up having the funeral, because they were waiting for people from Pennsylvania and all over to come in. It wasn't required that we go out there, but we still went just to check and make sure everything was still all right.

The day of the funeral, we don't go at all because of their religious beliefs, etc. There is no law that states that we have to be there during their funeral services. So they make their own caskets, perform their own funerals, dig their own graves, and bury the bodies. So, really, all they use a funeral home for is just the embalming part of the process.

Except for the embalming, they do everything else on their own. They started their own cemetery out in the country here in Logan County, and that's likely where they'll all be buried.

Bryson Price, Lewisburg, November 16, 2007

BODY HAULED FROM WASHINGTON STATE TO GLASGOW

People used to bury their own dead, and we had a situation just this past Saturday when they didn't bury their own, but they did transport the body of a family member. That has happened at least a couple of times. In one case, this fellow's uncle died in Washington State and wanted a funeral here in Glasgow. The nephew called us and said he'd be coming with his uncle's body.

I said, "Don't you want us to arrange transportation?"

He said, "No, my uncle worked that out, so I'll be bringing him myself."

So, it turned out he drove him from the state of Washington back to Glasgow. His uncle had told him when he died to go purchase a new pickup truck, put a camper top on the back of it, and after his body was embalmed for him to drive him back to Glasgow, and he could keep the pickup truck.

So, that's what he did!

Follis Crow, Glasgow, December 11, 2007

Treasures and More

We have placed in the caskets beer, cigarettes, and a lot of chewing to-bacco. There's been a lot of chewing tobacco stuck in the bibs of overalls or just inside their pants pockets. Several men have been buried in their bib overalls and work shirts. That's the way family members used to see them, so that's what we buried them in.

Sometimes we don't know what items are put in the casket by family members. A lot of times when they are going by the casket, they might slip in notes or remembrance items. Sometimes they put in model cars, special good-luck charms, flowers, etc. There's probably a half pint or two of whiskey slipped inside the casket at times.

Family members also put in the deceased person's hands such things as Bibles [or] flowers such as long-stem roses. Rosaries for Catholics are placed in their hands, and I've even seen dollar bills stuck in somebody's hand. We've also had a banjo placed in the hands of the corpse. The family was going to bury the banjo, and it was a very nice, expensive banjo. We kept the banjo in the casket during the visitation, but they did decide to take it out and keep it. Pocketknives have also been stuck in people's pockets because their favorite pocketknife has to be in their pocket.

Mainly with women, it is usually a rose, or pictures placed in the hands of the person's body or laid up next to their arms.

Stuffed animals, for both young and old, are also put in the caskets.

Follis Crow, Glasgow, December 11, 2007

Transporting the Body

Last weekend we had a death, and the family was going to have the burial in Missouri. They wanted us to make the removal at the hospital, embalm the body, and arrange for transportation. They asked me how I would transport the body.

I said, "Either by airplane or just drive over land."

So they got to figuring the cost. Then this lady said, "Well, I've got a Suburban. Will she fit in there?"

I said, "Well, yeah."

This man said, "Well, is it okay if I take her myself?"

I said, "Well, as far as I know there is no law against it." So we did the paperwork and off he went. He drove her to Missouri.

Follis Crow, Glasgow, December 11, 2007

AMISH FOLK CUSTOMS

We have local Amish families that do their own burials, etc. Doing that is always their tradition. A lot of times we do the embalming for the Amish; then they'll take the body back home and dress it.

Occasionally, the Amish don't embalm the bodies. There are some younger children that I've heard about for which some ice was packed in the casket if it's been a warm time of year. I don't think they keep them out an extended period of time.

Of course, they don't have to be embalmed, but lately we have embalmed several of the Amish family or Amish sect. We usually go get them, bring the body here and do the embalming, then take it back home. Usually one of their family members will come with us and stay here the whole time. Then we'll take the body back to the home and usually place them in a room on a board with some sawhorses out. Then they'll say, "We'll take it from here." And they do the dressing, put them in a casket which is homemade, then have the service and the burial.

So, they do their own.

Follis Crow, Glasgow, December 11, 2007

SERPENT-HANDLING BELIEVER

In our area here, we have a group of folks who are members of snake-handling churches. There are several stories about them. This lady that lived up the hollow, who found out she wasn't going to live very long, wanted to make a prearranged funeral. I went to her home; we went through everything. One of the things she emphasized the most was when she said, "Now, Brother Steele, everything is going to be at the church, and I want an old-time, spiritual-moving service. If the spirit moves them into handling serpents, I want them to handle serpents. I want an old-time church service for my funeral."

I said, "Well, I'll put that down, but you be sure and let the ministers know, too, so we can go ahead and fulfill your wishes."

Well, she lived about a year and a half before she passed away. The day of the service at the church, I couldn't find her husband or anybody in her family. I was just really amazed that they weren't there yet. So, I kept walking in and out of the church looking for them. Finally, I was walking out the back door of the church and looked and saw there in the very back row of the pews was her husband and family.

I backed up and said, "Brother XYZ, we reserved pews up in the front of the church for all family members to sit."

Brother XYZ looked up at me and said, "Now, Brother Steele, you and I know that she was a strong member of this church, and she believed in this faith and she handled serpents. She wants an old-time service, and you and I know that. She believed in handling them serpents, but we don't, so we're staying 'righch' here."

Jay Steele, Pineville, January 20, 2008

SNAKES IN GUITAR CASES

Bob Walden related to me about some of the ins and outs of snake-handling churches. One of them was that seldom do they actually come to the funeral home and handle serpents, part of that being that it is not a felony in the state of Kentucky but it is a misdemeanor to handle serpents. Well, the law enforcement is pretty easy when they're having services at the church, but when they have them at public places, like the funeral home, sometimes the law can get a little testy about things.

He was relating to me the story about the "untuned guitar" case. He said, "When they come into the funeral home, you watch all the guitars getting tuned up. And if there's a case that does not get opened, that's the case the snakes are in, and you want to be sure to watch that case to make sure that what comes in or goes out goes back in."

Jay Steele, Pineville, January 20, 2008

SERPENTS IN CASKETS

This Bob Walden shared with me information that when they are having funeral services, sometimes the spirit moves on ministers and the folks there in the church to place serpents in the casket with the deceased loved ones. Well, his favorite little thing he shared with me was that during the service, if you see the spirit move on them, they are going to pick up serpents to handle them, then start putting the serpents in the casket. He said, "You need to watch real close. You get to where you can see what's going in and out of that casket. And you need to count how many serpents they put in the casket, and then count how many serpents they take out of that casket. If they come up short one serpent, then that's when you need to get hold of the minister and tell him that he's going to close that casket."

Jay Steele, Pineville, January 20, 2008

The Way Things Used to Be

Some people still use the term "coffin," while virtually everyone knows them as caskets. I guess that's because we have gotten more commercial. It used to be that funeral directors would actually cover the wooden casket themselves, put on the wooden handles, and finish the interior. Thus, all they bought was a hull. And as far as size, there were many more sizes then than there are now. Basically, now there is more of a standard size for an adult and several different sizes for children.

They used to buy wooden caskets and then stack them into each other, then cover them with cloth, put the wood fiber in them, and then put the handles on. Things back then are a long ways from what they are like today. When I started work as a funeral director, things were already like they are today.

There were three firms in Louisville that made caskets. These were Fall City, National, and United casket companies. They actually made caskets and sold them in and around Louisville. All three are now out of business.

Before the days of embalming, a lot of people would die and then they were dressed and put in a casket, and their funeral would take place the next day.

I've heard stories about people that actually weren't dead but were just in a deep coma. I've not experienced anything like that because that's a day long gone. And there were stories about the dead person suddenly rising up in the casket. That took place back when there was a rigor mortis, which is a chemical change in the body that tightens the muscles. Sometimes that will make a leg move or some other body movement.

I've never seen this happen, but I've heard stories about it taking place back in the older days during horse-and-buggy times. And most of the people that were around during the years prior to embalming are now deceased. There are only a very few funeral directors still alive whom I know that are in their nineties.

And there are fewer and fewer numbers of funeral homes. In some towns where there used to be two or three, there might be just one now. It's the same way in bigger cities, where funeral homes have gotten bigger. It takes more and more to operate a funeral business now than it used to take years ago.

James R. Moraja Sr., Lebanon, March 28, 2008

MILITARY GRAVESIDE SERVICE

We had a military graveside service in a local cemetery on a very beautiful day. The widow wanted taps played, of course. Thus, the military troops then proceeded to play, as requested. The same lady who wanted taps played more than anything cried out, "That is the saddest song I have ever heard."

That was a very touching event.

Gregory Woodruff, Salem, March 17, 2008

LAST WORD

Some of the things we have buried with the remains include containers of Mountain Dew, shotguns and deer rifles (some of which are valued at two thousand dollars and more), photographs, valuable jewelry, extra false teeth and glasses, Rebel flags and knives, watches with alarms that would not stop, personal notes and letters, spare pocket change, and tobacco of all sorts.

I'm sure there are other items that I'm not aware of. And believe it or not, I guess if we could drive a U-Haul trailer on back of the hearse, somebody would request it!

Greg Woodruff, Salem, April 11, 2008

3

Funeral Humor and Mistakes

~

Humor often helps people cope with sad and difficult situations. Even when they are grief-stricken, bereaved relatives and friends of the deceased find comfort in remembering and retelling humorous stories about their loved ones. Funny stories and remarks also help people work through the stress of funeral services and burials. Funeral directors use humor among themselves, too, as a means of coping with the challenges of their profession.

The stories in this chapter feature humorous comments and misstatements at funeral services, bodies that move or go missing, deliberate pranks, falls and blunders, and family disagreements. The chapter also includes stories about embarrassing and distressing mistakes, some made by funeral directors and some made by the families they have served.

Whatever the focus of these tales, they provide meaningful insight into what family and community members face after a death and into what funeral directors face on a daily basis.

Death Due to Being Bathed

This event happened during the time when funeral homes still provided ambulance service to the county. The call came from out in the country asking for an ambulance for an older lady who was sick and needed to go to a hospital. She lived off the main roads, and so James Pendley and I met some people with a tractor and wagon and rode in that to this one-room log house out in the middle of a field. She was being cared for by her son. It was in the dead of winter and was extremely cold.

We saw this little old lady lying in bed, and we didn't think she had enough cover and would freeze before we got her to the ambulance. So we decided we would look for more blankets or quilts. We found a large number of quilts but they were all pinned together. It took us forever and a day to get a few of these quilts unpinned. We loaded her and all the quilts into the wagon and took her to the ambulance, then on to the Logan County Hospital. As we were going, James said, "They will kill this poor woman. They will bathe her, and she will be in that warm place. Her pores will open up and she will get pneumonia and die."

Well, three or four days later, we went back to the Logan County Hospital to pick her up, because she did die.

Back in those days, people didn't have running water in the house. They got their water from a spring or well. They also did not have bathrooms, and so not able to take full baths as often, especially in the wintertime. If they got sick enough to go to a hospital, while there they would be bathed and kept away from the environment they were used to, and around other sick people and in contact with new germs, and took pneumonia and couldn't fight it off, thus died.

I'm not exaggerating when I say there were probably seven or eight quilts on that sick little old lady that had been piled on her by us two young men.

A few years later we went back to that little one-room log house to pick up the son who had died there. And just like his mother before him, he was covered by many quilts, although not pieced together. It was winter again and was very, very cold, but we decided we didn't have to ride a wagon in to get him. We drove the hearse in to pick him up.

John A. Phelps, Bowling Green, with James M. Pendley,
Morgantown, March 3, 2008

NOT RUSHING

It used to be that when you went to the cemetery, people wanted to go directly to the grave and watch the casket being lowered. Funeral directors pretty much try to keep people from doing that now for safety reasons.

There was a family that had gathered around the grave, and one was crying very profusely, "I don't know what I'm going to do without you."

One other person said, "Does she want to go with them?" [Laughter]

I don't know if the person was in shock or not. But the tears dried, and there was silence from that moment on. I thought, now that was a devilish person that said that. But sometimes there are things people do when they are caught up in their grief, and they may say something that may call to their spirit that this is it. But the reality is that those of us that are on this side are not rushing to get to the other side.

Sometimes people associate hospice with the end of life, meaning that people are taking their last breath and are dying. There was a minister that said, "I understand when Mom or Dad die that you want to call a pastor and let him know that he can come and have prayer. But couldn't the pastor come at eight o'clock in the morning, and it would be as viable as opposed to three o'clock in the morning?"

There is nothing that a minister can truly do when there is a need for you to call and wake someone up out of their sleep to say their loved one is gone. So the inclination is that "You must come, and you must have prayer with us."

We can certainly understand that, but can prayer be done over the phone, or do you physically have to go to the person that called?

This was not a story, but it tells about things that take place.

Gayle Graham, Louisville, May 1, 2008

WIDOW THREATENS TO SHORTEN THE PREACHER'S COMMENTS

The funeral profession, like the doctoral profession, demands that these people have got to learn a lot of respect. My dad earned a lot of respect from his dealings, which kind of rubbed off on me. However, I don't reckon I ever had a fight during a funeral that I know of, but if there's any family friction it comes out during a funeral.

This happened not too long ago. A fellow had been in a hospital down in Bowling Green, and he died while there. He wanted this chaplain to conduct the funeral, and the chaplain got over to talk with the man's wife. She said, "There is one thing. He lived his life the way he wanted to and I respect him for it, so I don't want a long eulogy delivered. So, one thing, Preacher, if I stick my finger up, it's time for you to wind up." [Heavy laughter]

I don't know if the widow stuck her finger up or not, but the preacher didn't stay up there too long. I was standing there when she told him that. She wasn't up to sitting there for an hour and a half listening to somebody talk for so long, as she was tired riding back and forth from the hospital. But her comments were certainly unexpected on his part.

Charles McMurtrey, Summer Shade, July 29, 2007

A Twisting Casket

Shortly after I got my embalmer's license, Silas Norris over in Burkesville wasn't a licensed embalmer, so I'd go over and embalm anybody that needed it. The casket had a kind of spring affair that you could raise up and down. And Norris had the body in this casket in which something moved around, and the casket tilted a little bit. I asked Dad to clarify this, and here is what he added. "The spring broke or come loose and the inside shifted, causing the body to tilt. When he opened the lid, the body wasn't laying in there the right way." Of course, that upset the family, and him too! [Laughter] So, we had to go get him and bring him back to the funeral home so that he could swap caskets.

Well, that embarrassed him, but the family members didn't think the casket's movement had woke the deceased up from the dead.

Charles McMurtrey, Summer Shade, July 29, 2007

Copperhead Snake at the Funeral

This story is about Mr. Buddy Cox. He told me about a funeral they had at Red Hill. They were having a committal service. He and his son were there, and the minister was conducting the funeral service. Cox's son looked down and saw this copperhead snake right at his feet. He couldn't holler or jump, so he just put his foot on the snake's head and held it there till the preacher got done!

Billy Dowell, Mt. Vernon, August 27, 2007

Mugging for the Camera

Funeral director Cox had a 742-pound woman in his care, and Brother Harvey Pensol preached her funeral there at the funeral home. Well, Brother Harvey stood up there and was getting ready to have the service when this woman's daughter stood up and sort of shrieked out, "Hey, wait just a minute; stop everything."

She went up there and said, "Take my picture now." [Laughter]

So they had to wait for the cameras to stop flashing.

Billy Dowell, Mt. Vernon, August 27, 2007

HATS OFF AND BOLOGNA FRISBEE

Another funeral Buddy Cox had was preached at by Brother Harvey. When the funeral ceremony was going on, a grandson or some other member of the family was sitting there with his hat on.

An elderly lady yelled, "Get that damn hat off," then slapped him up beside the head! [Laughter]

They had brought about a half roll of bologna to the funeral, and they were passing it back and forth like throwing a Frisbee. They would cut a slice of it off, then toss it around.

Billy Dowell, Mt. Vernon, August 27, 2007

KOTEX OR KODAK

Here's a story I like to tell. We had this man laid out at the funeral home. His widow wanted a two-night visitation, but on the second day there wasn't anybody there except the body and the widow and me.

I was sitting in the lounge area and the widow came in. She was chewing her gum just as hard as she could. She said to me, "Mr. Dowell, have you got a Kotex?"

She was probably in her late seventies, so I thought as to why in the world did she want a Kotex.

Well, that was before the days of enlightenment, when you didn't talk about those things. So, I could just feel my face getting hot and red. I said, "No ma'am, I don't have a Kotex."

She was really chewing that gum and said, "Well, [I] wonder where I could get one."

The man that worked for us lived upstairs, and his wife was pregnant and didn't figure she had any need for one. I said, "Well, one of them women over there at the flower shop might have one."

She said, "Well, I was just wondering. I was wanting some pictures made."

I didn't have the heart to tell her she wanted a Kodak camera!

Billy Dowell, Mt. Vernon, August 27, 2007

HEAVY DRINKER FELL INTO GRAVE

They've always told this, but I can't prove it; nor do I doubt that it happened. Back prior to 1952 when it was Cox Funeral Home, they were going to bury somebody over at the Elwood Cemetery here in town. They went in and dug the grave the day before the service, and there was a man here in town whose name was Josh Frederick. He had a habit of drinking a little too much, so he got on a bender and was walking home through the cemetery, and he fell in a grave and passed out. He wasn't hurt, but he laid there all night. He woke up the next morning when the sun was coming up. He looked around and said, "Vell, vell, resurrection morning and I'm the firstun up."

Billy Dowell, Mt. Vernon, August 27, 2007

ST. PETER AND THE PREACHER

We were having a funeral and everybody there were sad. So, the preacher had a captive audience and he was going to preach to them. He got to telling about the Apostle Peter, what a great man he was; about Peter denying Jesus three times; then after the resurrection how Peter stood in and healed the sick, and this and that. He talked about what a great man Peter was by establishing his Church on the Rock. The preacher then said, "Just think what the Lord could have done if he had had two Peters."

Well, those people that had got so sad, they got so tickled they couldn't hardly stand it. You could see them a-shaking. There was one woman there that just blowed up. She couldn't hold it any longer. She just laughed out big and loud because she thought the preacher had said "two peters."

I don't know whether the preacher realized what he said, or not! [Laughter]

Billy Dowell, Mt. Vernon, August 27, 2007

SNAKE IN CHURCH

We had another church funeral. It was a rural church. It was warm weather, but they didn't have the air conditioner on. They just left the front door to the church open. The preacher was up there in the pulpit having the service when a snake crawled in the door. This fellow there in the congregation saw the snake, then said aloud, "Hellfire, there's a damn snake!" Then he jumped right up into the pew!

Billy Dowell, Mt. Vernon, August 27, 2007

TEENAGE PRANKSTERS

Around the year 1880, Thomps Goodman had a hotel in Fountain Run. A traveling salesman stopped in for the night. During his stay the salesman died, so the townspeople laid the salesman out upon the counter. As it was a custom back then, the local people sat up all night with him.

During the night, some local boys made a ruckus outside. The people ran into the street to see what was going on. While they were outside, some boys slipped into the hotel and took the salesman out of the room, and one of the boys laid down on the counter in the salesman's place.

Everyone came back in and got settled a bit. But before long, the boy under the sheet started moaning. Well, that scared all the people. Some screamed, some left, and some almost fainted. But the boys had a good laugh at the expense of the poor dead salesman.

Connie Hughes Goodman, Fountain Run, September 11, 2007

FUNERAL DIRECTOR'S PRANK

My father, James Hughes, was working for another funeral home in Kentucky and the proprietor had a crush on Susie, a waitress at the local café. Mr. Q, I'll call him, came one day and was bragging that after two years he'd finally managed to get Susie to go out with him.

Dad inquired as to where he'd been taking her.

Mr. Q said, "The movies," then went on doing his daily routine.

Dad thought it would be quite humorous to pull a prank on the couple. So he soaked a wad of cotton from the morgue in formaldehyde and strategically placed it in Mr. Q's car heater.

That blissful night of courtship for Mr. Q went really well. They went to the movies and then to the ice cream shop for a malt shake. The night air became cool and Susie expressed that she felt chilled. Mr. Q obliged her by turning the heater on. The odor from the embalming fluid flooded the car with a stench that would burn your eyeballs right out of their sockets.

I don't know if Susie ever went out with Mr. Q again, but Dad still gets a chuckle when he tells that tale.

Connie Hughes Goodman, Fountain Run, September 11, 2007

FUNERAL DIRECTOR'S POCKETKNIFE

The funniest things can happen, even happen at funerals. When all is quiet and everyone is looking on, strange things can happen. For example, my grandfather took a body to Akersville to be laid out at church, and when he got there, everyone was waiting patiently, and the casket lid would not open. It was shut good and tight. Grandfather fumbled at it for a while. Without panicking, although the perspiration was surely exposed, he reached into his pocket and got his pocketknife. He carefully pried open the lid with the knife. Later on, a man said to Grandfather, "Edison, I thought I was going to have to come and help you!" [Laughter]

Connie Hughes Goodman, Fountain Run, September 11, 2007

LADY'S SENIOR MOMENT

Another cute story is one I was talking about to a friend of mine the other day. He told me his grandmother was in her nineties, and her two sons, who were this man's dad and uncle, had been fairly closely associated in different things in this community. They decided to go buy their cemetery lots for themselves and their families. So they bought the lots all together in the Memorial Gardens.

Their mother was not used to the memorial-type gardens with flat, unseen stones. So, they decided to take her over there one Sunday. They took her out to eat, then took her over to show her the cemetery plots. But she intended to be buried with her deceased husband in another county from which they originally came, thus was not to be buried in Memorial Gardens.

She made the remark to them, "I guess this is okay, but I don't know how in the world I could ever find your-all's graves when I come to visit." [Laughter]

She wasn't a stupid person by any means; that was just the first thing that came to her mind, "How in the world am I going to find your-all's graves?"

She was in her early nineties, and they were probably approaching sixty, maybe a year or so older.

William Bledsoe, Irvine, September 26, 2007

OTHER NAMES FOR PALLBEARERS

I was in the office by myself back when I was in my twenties. It was a rather quiet day. We had a service that was to start in the afternoon, but this happened around nine or ten o'clock that morning. Not much was going on, as people were not coming in or out. This lady interrupted my thoughts there in front of the door to my office. I heard her say, "Do you have a car for the ball bearings?"

I wondered if I heard her right; maybe I misunderstood, and I said, "Ma'am?"

She said, "Well, my son is going to be a ballbearer, and I wondered if you had a car for them."

I then realized that he was a pallbearer. Believe it or not, I've heard people say "pallparrots," "pallbearings," and every name in the world. Their words would rhyme, or were in rhythm, with "pallbearer."

William Bledsoe, Irvine, September 26, 2007

DEAD MAN TALKING

I had a man back when I was in my twenties laid out here in the funeral home. I was by myself, quiet. He was from another community but had been brought back here since he was from here originally. I didn't know who his girlfriend was, thus knew nothing about her as she was not from here. She came into the office here and said, "Mister, I want you to come up here to the casket. He's trying to tell me something."

I asked her, "Well, what is he doing?"

She said, "He's trying to open his mouth, and he's trying to flutter his eyes."

I told her that I would go to the casket with her. And while I was going up, I kept thinking, "Lady, don't get in my way, because if he is fluttering his eyes and trying to open his mouth, I want to clear this building."

William Bledsoe, Irvine, September 26, 2007

WIDOW WITH BOYFRIEND

Harold Hunt was a funeral director here in Irvine for years and also a former mayor of Irvine. He was considerably older than I am. I'm sixty now, and Harold would be around eighty-four if he were still living. He is who I started working with from almost day one, and we became very close friends. Harold was one of the most likable individuals you'll ever know—a big cut-up and a lot of fun to be around and a jack of all trades. He had never been licensed as a funeral director but had always worked in the funeral business. I think at that time that I was already licensed, and he did get his license before he died.

We had a funeral of a gentleman who had been in a mental institution. He had no family except his widow, and they had not been together for years and years. We prepared him, and in the arrangements, because of the limitation of funds, etc., we may have been doing his funeral preparations free, gratis; I can't remember. Anyway, we were to meet at the cemetery where he was to be buried. We had a tent set and was going to have a short graveside service. Well, the only two people that appeared were his widow, who was a little old lady, very backward. I don't mean this in any way except that she was just sort of a funny-type person. And she had a boyfriend who was equally so. She was actually living with him, but they were quite elderly.

The minister, Mr. Hunt, and myself were the only ones there, with the exception of the man who was preparing the grave. I can remember looking up, and here came his widow and her boyfriend. Both of them were not very big people and probably didn't weigh more than 110 pounds each. Actually, I doubt if she weighed ninety pounds. They were not the best-kept people in the world, such as clean. We brought them into the tent and they sat in two chairs right in front of the casket. The minister came forward and spoke, and I was standing in one side of the tent at what would be the foot of the casket and to those two persons' right. Mr. Hunt was standing at what would be off-center to the head of the casket to their left on the far side of the tent.

We opened the casket after the service so she could see her husband, then moved back in the positions we were in originally. She sat there in the chair and looked at her husband for a while, then looked over at her boyfriend and called him by name. She asked him, "Do you think it would be okay if I went over and kissed him?"

He said, "You can do whatever you want to, but it will make your lips sore."

And he said that in such a way that you could tell he did not want her kissing him, because it was more a mark of jealousy than it was a concern for her lips.

I looked down at the tips of the toes of my shoes, and it was all I could do to keep from bursting out laughing. I dared not look up because I knew that if I saw Harold Hunt's eyes, I'll lose it, and he will too, probably.

Someway after the service, both of us had to go someplace. I don't know where it was, but I think we just about died from laughter.

I believe if I live to be three hundred years old, that's the funniest damn thing that I ever experienced in the funeral business. She did kiss him, but I never looked. Once he said that, it wasn't funny when she said, "Would it be okay to kiss him?" It would not have been funny to me if she had kissed him. What was funny was his remark back to her, and what I interpreted to be exactly what he meant by it. "I don't want you kissing him, dead or alive. You are mine now. Whatever use you are to me, you are mine."

William Bledsoe, Irvine, September 26, 2007

NONPAYING CUSTOMER

I had a lady one time that wouldn't pay, and my boss said, "Well, ma'am, you owe me the money, and you've made no effort to pay me whatsoever."

She said, "What you need is competition."

He said, "Well, what would competition have to do with it?"

She said, "Well, we'd have a choice as to where to go."

He said, "Well, you wouldn't go long. You're not going to pay them either, are you?"

William Bledsoe, Irvine, September 26, 2007

GOOD SERMON MATERIAL

Brother Compton, pastor of Severns Baptist Church, is from Canmer, Hart County. We've been out together at funeral services, and he tells me every time I'm with him that I'm good sermon material! [Laughter]

I don't know how to take that exactly, but I take it okay! We have a good time together.

Bob Brown, Elizabethtown, September 25, 2007

KEEPING FUNERAL HOME DOOR CLEAN

One thing I remember about Logan Dixon, in the Dixon-Atwood-Adkins Funeral Home here in Elizabethtown, is that he had a lot of irons in the fire and was in and out all the time. One thing I remember about him is that he would always come in the door and say, "Well, is that front door clean? That front door needs to be kept clean, so keep the fingerprints off that door." He'd laugh and say, "Because somebody might come in and say, 'I wonder if they washed Mamaw's feet?'"

We always made sure the door was clean when he came in, because if there were fingerprints on the door, he'd come in and say that.

Bob Brown, Elizabethtown, September 25, 2007

E-TOWN SANTA CLAUS

We have a man that's still living here in E-town, and they call him Santa Claus. He drives a red pickup truck, he wears a red suit, and he has a white beard. He's made his own casket and it is in his living room right now, this very minute. And he's going to be buried in that casket whenever he dies. Right now it's also a coffee table, and they use it for that purpose in the front room of his house. It's wood, either oak or cherry.

Everybody calls him Santa Claus, including his own family! He's quite a guy, too—pretty colorful.

Bob Brown, Elizabethtown, September 25, 2007

TONGUE-TIED SINGER

Some of the times when a body was taken back home, even when I started practice, people didn't have electricity. We'd take car batteries for the lighting and alligator clips. We'd go out, and neighbors would come in and set up all night. Then they'd have a couple of songs before you went to the church for the funeral.

On one occasion, they called on this guy to lead us in a song. Well, I knew this guy and I knew he couldn't talk plain at all. I thought maybe he was like Mel Tillis, and he could sing okay. The first song he started out with was "When the Tanks Go Marchin' In."

I think that would tickle anybody, but I was just a sixteen-year-old kid and I couldn't stand his voice. While he was singing that song tongue-tied, I got to laughing, and I fell off this great big porch right into an apple tree! Then that got the other funeral director that was with me tickled. We like to have broken up a good funeral, but we got through it all right.

That's one of my first remembrances of a funny story in this business.

Terry Dabney, Campbellsville, October 13, 2007

Singing out of Turn

I know of a guy who used to go to our local hospital and sing to patients. But he didn't ever think about whether they were real sick or not. He'd sing "We'll Miss You When You're Gone." There are some funny stories about that!

Terry Dabney, Campbellsville, October 13, 2007

Lady Finally Stopped Talking

There's any number of humorous stories I've seen in this business. One that strikes me is about a nephew that was making arrangements on his aunt. He came in to see her after we had everything ready. He looked over at her, then said, "Ha, that's the quietest I ever saw her." [Laughter]

That just struck me funny! And if you knew the person that was in the casket, you'd understand that. She was always talking.

Terry Dabney, Campbellsville, October 16, 2007

She Up and Died

Here's a story about this man whose wife died. Their marriage was the second one for both of them. They'd been married four or five years. He said, "About the time I was getting used to her, she up and died." [Laughter]

He didn't mean for that to be funny; that's just the way it was. But it just struck us here in the funeral home as really funny.

Terry Dabney, Campbellsville, October 13, 2007

SONG FOR DEAD HUSBAND

There's all kinds of things that have happened. In one instance, the wife had kicked her husband out of the house. So when we asked the family what songs her dead husband liked, or what songs he'd like to have played and sung at the funeral, they said to play and sing "Where Am I Going to Live When I Get Home?" [Laughter]

Terry Dabney, Campbellsville, October 16, 2007

OOPS, AN ARCH

One time we had a flat tire on the hearse going to the cemetery. That in itself wasn't funny, but where we arrived there was a deaf-mute [person] that lived there. He was out there trying to tell us all about what to do. Of course, none of us could understand what he said. I had called for another vehicle to come so as to get us on to the cemetery, which we finally did.

Of course, in a situation like that, five minutes seems like fifty. We got over to the cemetery, and just after the funeral service there, we looked and there was a pond in the cemetery. Well, a man was over there using the bathroom in this pond in front of God and everybody. The preacher looked over at him and said, "Oops, he's trying to show us his arch, isn't he!" [Laughter]

That just seemed funny to us that the preacher would come up with something like that.

Terry Dabney, Campbellsville, October 13, 2007

STUNNED INTO SILENCE

I knew a preacher really well, and he talked all the time, a lot more than I do, and faster. You couldn't shut him up for nothing. It was really wet one time when we were doing a funeral, and me and him fell down into the grave after the family left. I have often said that's the only time I ever heard that preacher shut up! When he fell in the grave, he didn't have a thing to say! He was just stunned. [Laughter]

Terry Dabney, Campbellsville, October 13, 2007

Hollering Palsy

There was a woman that used to come all the time to funerals, and she would just holler out really loud, "Oops, oops," during the funeral while the preacher was preaching.

We got tired of listening to her, so we asked her one time why she did that. She said, "I've got hollering palsy."

That's the only case of hollering palsy I've ever heard, but that's what she said she had. I didn't believe her and still don't, but that may be right.

Terry Dabney, Campbellsville, October 13, 2007

Check as Good as Cash

In the caskets we put things such as tobacco, fishing poles, cards, and whiskey. We buried one person who had two-karat diamond rings put in her casket. We buried just about anything you can imagine with people's bodies. We've never buried cash, but I've been trying my best to get somebody to take their cash with them. Then I'd put a check in the casket, and if that check ever came through the bank, I'd honor it. That wouldn't be dishonest, would it; just take my cash out and put my check in there? I've never got that arranged yet! I'm still working on that. [Heavy laughter]

Terry Dabney, Campbellsville, October 13, 2007

Five Times Dead

One time the local hospital called me five times in one day to come pick up the same person that had been pronounced dead five times by a licensed physician. And every time, he had come back to life before I got there.

So, that got to be a joke, as you can imagine. I never did know the story of that, but I told them the last time, when they finally did say he was dead and I could pick him up, I said, "Well, do you think I should have a hammer with me handy, in case something happens again and he comes back to life?" [Laughter]

But he didn't. He stayed dead that time!

Terry Dabney, Campbellsville, October 13, 2007

GETTING REPEAT BUSINESS

I think people sometimes deal with death in different ways. I guess when they criticize funeral directors, they probably do it to themselves but usually just don't call again. My daddy, who was also a funeral director, said, "The way to have a good business is to have repeat business."

This lady that I have right now, whom I am going to have visitation with tomorrow, I buried her grandparents, her parents, and her brothers and sisters. So the way to have a good funeral business is to have that repeat business. It's like Daddy said, "People can call you once, but they don't have to call you the second time." So I've tried to always adhere to what he said.

A bunch of funeral directors were at a coroners' in-service training one day, and we all went out to eat. This fellow and I were sitting there talking, along with some others, so he and I were laughing. He said, "When I was taking my state board examination, one of the questions they asked was, 'Do you know what a funeral director is?'"

He said, "Oh, yeah. A funeral director is a person that kisses your behind while you're alive so that they can wipe it when you're dead."

The guy on the state board said, "Well, I guess that's a pretty good answer!"

I used the term "behind," but that wasn't what he said. The term he used was a three-letter word that begins with an *a*. [Heavy laughter]

Rayfield Houghlin, Bloomfield, October 17, 2007

KENTUCKY'S FINEST

I guess one of the cutest stories that I can remember is about taking people home. There used to be a liquor store across the street from our funeral home. We had a person here that had died, and we were taking her up to the house. We were taking her to her mother-in-law's place.

Well, this fellow had really serious problems, as he really liked to drink.

I forget exactly what time we were going to have this lady laid out at home.

I was only fourteen or fifteen years old at the time. I went up there and we walked into the house, and this fellow said to my daddy, "Mr. Buck, if I had known you were going to be here this early, I'd let you to have brought me a drink." He called my daddy Mr. Buck.

He said that because he knew we were right across the street from the liquor store. I can remember Daddy saying to him, "Who moved all this furniture out of here? Did anybody help you?"

He said, "Mr. Buck, I've carried so much furniture, I feel like I've miscarriaged." [Laughter] And the funny thing was, here were his wife and all her family sitting around. Of course, this fellow didn't care because that's just the way he was. Whatever came to his mind, that's just what he was going to say. As a matter of fact, when he died, I had his funeral, and his family put a bottle of Kentucky's Finest in the casket with him.

In another situation, he came in here one time, and he was sitting right here in this chair that I'm in right now. I was over in another chair a few feet away from him. When he walked in here, he said, "Field, what does it cost to be created?"

I said, "Created? I don't know what you're talking about."

He said, "When I die, I want to be created."

I again said, "I don't know what you're talking about."

He said, "Oh, goddammit, that's when they burn your a_ _ up."

I said, "You mean you want to be cremated!"

Of course, he had been across the street there in the whiskey store before he came over here to visit with me.

He always had a lot of good stories, and he had a lot of fun.

Another time he asked me if, when he died, if I would do him a favor. I said, "Well, if I can I will."

He said, "Well, will you go up to the hardware store and get a spigot and some copper tubing and run it down in the ground and put it in my mouth? Every once in a while you all come along and pour a half pint in the spigot for me." [Laughter]

He was truly quite a guy. He was a brick mason and laid all kinds of rocks and could have been worth a lot of money. He worked hard and did a good job, but he had a little problem with alcohol.

Rayfield Houghlin, Bloomfield, October 17, 2007

DEAD HUNTER RAISES SHOULDER

Sometimes when you start the injection of fluid, especially if the body is real warm, you may get a slight reaction of the legs, or maybe the fingers, but very seldom of anything else.

In one incident, this started happening with the shoulders raising up. This guy was a hunter who was used to raising his gun up. So I think that was one of the very few times that I've ever witnessed that type thing! [Laughter]

William Lee Shannon, Shelbyville, October 25, 2007

NOT LOST

We've had a lot of colorful ministers that were very loud, very emotional, very animated in their movements, and would run the length of the floor in the chapel, start in one end and go to the other. We had one loud service one day. One of our gravediggers had been helping the man that digs the graves. He said, "That reminded me of our revival when I was a kid. That preacher was just like the one that came storming all the way up the aisle to the back of the church at that time. He pointed his finger at me and said, 'Son, are you lost?'"

He was about ten years old at that time, and he said, "No, sir. I just live about a half mile down the road." [Laughter]

Follis Crow, Glasgow, December 11, 2007

BUSINESS LOOKING UP

There are all kinds of jokes about us. People will ask, "Are you busy?" Or, they will especially ask, "How's business?"

They expect us to say, "Well, it's pretty dead!"

But I've often said, "It's looking up!"

Follis Crow, Glasgow, December 11, 2007

HAND FROM BEHIND

This is a funny story that happened to the minister not too long ago. Sometimes ministers will ride in the hearse with me to the cemetery, but most times they'll drive their own car.

This minister here in Glasgow, Steve Higginbotham, is a big tall fellow and a nice guy. He got into the hearse with us, was sitting down, and as we pulled out he reached over his shoulder to grab the seat belt to put it on. Well, in the funeral hearse there is a glass partition between the front part where the passengers ride and the back where the casket is.

When he reached over his shoulder to get the seat belt, he saw the reflection of his hand in the glass partition behind him. He yelled and jerked back and jerked down like somebody was grabbing him.

That was one of the funniest things that ever happened, and he and I still get a kick out of what happened. He thought somebody was back there getting ready to get him.

Follis Crow, Glasgow, December 11, 2007

That's All She Wrote

This is a funny story that comes to my mind quite often. It happened in a church in recent years. The father of a fairly good friend of mine died, and one of my directors and I were at a church.

I guess one of the worst things you could do at a funeral, at least in front of a family or friends, is to get to laughing and tickled about something. That happened to me in church occasionally. We'd sit down on one of the front pews and get to laughing about something, then couldn't stop. If you finally got to giggling, you just couldn't stop.

Well, we were at a church in Monroe County, and we had passed everyone by the casket to have their final view. The family had gone up last to have their final viewing of the body of this fairly young man who was in his fifties or sixties. So, they were all fairly emotional, and we were just as somber as we usually are.

Larry, who was one of the other funeral directors, and I went up to close the casket. It was wintertime, and everybody had remained in the church. They didn't go outside after viewing. The church was full of people, and the family was sitting right by us on the front row.

So Larry held the floor blanket, and I closed the lid. As I pushed the lid, just at the last second as I closed it, a son said, "Oh, that's all she wrote."

You've got to know that fellow. He's very country in his speech, and when he said, "That's all she wrote," it hit me and Larry, and I was biting my lip and my tongue in order to keep from bursting out laughing right there. I looked over at Larry, and his face was turning red. He was ready to lose it, too!

Luckily, we got out of there without embarrassing ourselves by laughing. But that fellow said, "That's all she wrote," and he was serious, too.

Follis Crow, Glasgow, December 11, 2007

Voice from the Grave

This is one of my premier stories from the past about ordinary and extraordinary people I have known during my lifetime. This man was from over in the direction of Caneyville, Grayson County. He could do tricks with his voice, called "throwing a voice." (We know this as ventriloquism now.) It was pretty spooky. Few had even heard of him, and I don't think anyone there knew him.

He was among the crowd at the grave site for the funeral service. I don't think others there knew this man, nor heard of him.

Back then, our equipment for the cemetery work was not as fancy as we have now. We now use straps to let the casket down into the grave using a mechanical device. But at that time, men in the community where the deceased lived would use ropes under each end of the casket to let it down, little by little. It was hard on backs, knees, and hands to do this, but it had to be done.

Well, these pallbearers started lowering the casket, letting the ropes out a little at a time. When they did that, this fellow in the crowd threw his voice down in the grave and said in a rough, grumbly voice, "Let me down easy, boys."

When he said those words, the pallbearers dropped the ropes, casket and all, and they left the scene and didn't come back. Some people in the crowd that were closest to the grave also heard the voice from the grave, and they backed away. I've always wondered if they talked about that day or if they kept quiet.

That was all of it! That burial was over in a hurry.

James M. Pendley, Morgantown, March 3, 2008

Understatement

We had a visitation in this funeral home ten or fifteen years ago. Gene Vaughan, who is my colleague here, is married to Evelyn, who is a real Southern lady. She has only good things to say about any and all people. She was opening the front door for people as they came in, and there was a brother and sister that walked up, and just as they got to the door the elastic in the sister's underwear broke and her panties fell!

She just stepped down, picked them up, put them in her purse, looked at Evelyn and said, "Well, I've never had that to happen before."

Evelyn looked at her and said, "Neither have I."

The point of this story is the understatement of the century. When they got ready to leave, she looked at her brother and said, "George, have you got your hat? Don't you lose your hat."

She had lost her panties, but she was worried about his hat! [Laughter]

John A. Phelps, Bowling Green, March 3, 2008

The Great Pretender

I guess you'd call us salespersons. But most all of us never tried to sell the family anything. Most of the time, when they come in, they have in mind the amount of money they want to spend. And if you'll get out of there, they'll pretty well take care of that and stay within their financial means. That's the best practice I think anybody could do.

One time we had two visitations going on. We had this guy from the Wingfield community who was a character. At that time, everybody sat up at the funeral home. But when we had the person laid out, nobody stayed there.

John [pseudonym] knew about what time this family was going to come in for the viewing. Without me knowing about it or anything, we had lights off in there, and he crawled in behind the casket. When they came in and we turned the lights on, somebody walked up there real close and was viewing the body and talked about how good they looked. John started talking to them behind the casket!

He said that was going pretty well, but he just thought how funny it would be to grab one of them. So he grabbed one by the ankle and said something else to them, called them by name. Well, that poor lady he grabbed like to have died!

I just about shot him when I found out what he had done, but he was still laughing hard about it. But all others there was just fine once they found out what was going on. They got a big kick out of it.

Jerry B. Patton, Brownsville, March 3, 2008

Just Departed

I was seventeen years old when I first started in this business. We had a lady there at the funeral home that had been killed in a car wreck. I had been standing there talking to a lady when another one called. These are not their real names, but I'll call them Mary and Marion Johnson.

This lady that called wanted to know if we had Marion Johnson there. I thought she was talking about Mary, the lady I was talking to, so I said, "No, she just left."

Then she said, "John, I know you all do good work, but I don't think your work is that good!" [Laughter]

John A. Phelps, Bowling Green, March 3, 2008

WISHFUL SPEAKING

This lady that worked for us was in the old block building in which we were located at that time. She was sitting there during one of those days when everyone was running their legs off and were just wild crazy. The phone rang and she said, "Sharer Funeral Home."

The person that called asked, "Is John [pseudonym of dead person] there?"

She said, "Yeah, do you want to speak to him?" [Heavy laughter]

Well, she realized what she had done, so she just eased the phone over on the receiver and turned it loose. Her face got red. She said, "I have made a fool out of myself."

Jerry B. Patton, Brownsville, March 3, 2008

SINGING ONE'S PART

I was involved in funeral service at Boyd Funeral Home in Salem, Livingston County. I don't recall the name of the deceased person for whom we were having service, but I vividly recall the two ministers who were there, one to do the formal service, the other in charge of the music. These ministers were Reverend Harley Rose and Reverend "Tootie" Harris.

The family of the deceased selected the music, while both ministers selected the full order of service. Reverend Rose said to the music minister, "Play the song 'Only a Rose Will Do'; then I will do my part." He went on to say, "Then play 'How Great Thou Art,' and that will be your part."

Both ministers burst out laughing, as the song selections indeed promoted a good sense of humor.

Gregory Woodruff, Salem, March 1, 2008

Grief Bumped Aside

We had a case in which the money to pay for the funeral was hard to come by. One of the children had caused many problems, one of which was vowing not to pay a dime on the funeral bill. The lady was standing at the casket when the funeral service was over, just viewing. She was dressed in tight shorts with a T-shirt that said "Life is a Racket."

Well, she was no spring chick, a very fiftyish woman. The casket for this service was what some people in our area called a Georgia Copper, or Cloth-Covered, because some families that used them had little or no money.

This woman proceeded to put on a show, including wailing, fake tears, etc. Well, she bumped the casket with her leg, and the lid bumped against the wall and fell. It hit the lady right on top of her head. We had never seen "grief" leave someone so very quickly.

I looked around to my boss, Mr. Boyd, and he was smiling because he knew her mournful sounds were fakes.

Gregory Woodruff, Salem, March 17, 2008

Rolling Out the Red Carpet

We had a death at Western State Hospital in Hopkinsville. As we stopped the hearse around in the back of the building, we noticed a woman standing close to where we parked. We proceeded to remove the cot from the back of the hearse. As we always did, we folded a red piece of carpet over the bumper to keep the legs of the cot from scratching the bumper.

The woman asked who we had come to pick up. We told her we did not know, thinking it might be someone she knew. She then said something very funny, "They must be awfully damn important since you are rolling out the red carpet for them!"

Something we thought very little about was noticed by someone with mental illness.

Gregory Woodruff, Salem, March 17, 2008

Great Balls of Fire

We were having a funeral committal service at the grave site, and rain was really coming down. All was well, but after the minister's prayer started, lightning hit the metal tent frame. When that happened, a blue fire ran around the large area of tent frame where everyone could see it. I don't remember whether or not the minister ever said amen, because everyone left in a rush!

Gregory Woodruff, Salem, March 17, 2008

FUNERAL DIRECTOR'S SHOWMANSHIP

There was a funeral director that was always flamboyant. I'd say he had showmanship; that's what I would call it. When a funeral director dies, it is customary for those funeral directors that are in the area to attend the service, just to give honor to another funeral director. His funeral was one of those type funerals.

We were there, and the funeral directors were in their area. The person that was conducting the service was a close friend to the person that died.

The family came in and a lot of others that knew this individual, who had done a lot in the community. The family members were not somber, but they were quiet. Then, a lot of the dead man's employees came in, and all of them were just wailing, "Oh, I can't believe; I can't believe; I just can't believe."

While they were wailing, a funeral director turned around and looked, then put his hand up and said, "Until you all can get yourself together, step to the side and let the rest of the people in."

That was probably the most comical thing, but it was funny. The family came in, and I think he thought at first that he was the head of the family, and that maybe some of the family members have come a little disconnected. But when he turned around and saw who it was, he just went back and put his hands up just like you do to stop traffic and to say, "Until you all can get yourself together, step to the side and let the other people in."

To me, that was funny! It didn't disrupt the service; it was just that he was that brave to do something like that. So I thought, Now that's real showmanship!

Gayle Graham, Louisville, May 1, 2008

MISTAKEN IDENTITY?

They always told the story about this gentleman that passed away, and he had three or four children and his wife. They came to the funeral, and the preacher was up there and he just kept preaching, telling them what a great fellow this man was and all the wonderful things he had done for the community.

The widow said to her children, "You all go up there to the casket to make sure that's your dad he's talking about." [Heavy laughter]

Denny Northcutt, Morehead, May 7, 2008

Weird Dog Sounds

I was a partner in another funeral home before I built this one. We were having a visitation here, and two women came in the office and said, "That body is making a noise."

I said, "There's no way that body could be making a noise," and I went in to check on things and there wasn't anything happening. I went back in the office and they came back in and said, "You need to come in here. Something is wrong. He is making a noise."

Well, what had happened was that a dog had gotten under the floor and was having pups. And it did sound that way! [Laughter]

So I had to get the town loafer to come by, and I gave him five dollars to crawl under the funeral home to get those pups and that mother dog out from underneath the porch.

Denny Northcutt, Morehead, May 7, 2008

Bodies Delivered to Wrong Sites

Mr. Cox, a funeral director here, told me this tale, and I personally remember this happening. He was supposed to get a body out of Detroit, I believe. At least, it was from some place quite a distance from here. They were going to fly it into Lexington. He went over there and met the plane, loaded the body up, brought it back, opened it up, and this black woman was in the casket. He was supposed to be getting a white man's body.

They had a terrible mix up. The woman was supposed to go to Alabama, but I think the white man went to Alabama instead. So, the woman's body was here in Mt. Vernon.

Well, they got hold of the airline and finally got it worked out, but it was a real hassle though.

Billy Dowell, Mt. Vernon, August 27, 2007

A Stingy Fellow

There is a story about a curious fellow who liked to save his money. He was a bachelor and lived with his mother. His poor, fragile mother died at home, and instead of him calling the funeral home to come and get her, he just put her in the car, buckled her in, and drove her to the funeral home himself.

He said he was just being helpful and didn't want the expense of the pick up charge. I wonder how he felt to find out that we don't have a pick up charge.

Connie Hughes Goodman, Fountain Run, September 11, 2007

Not a Ghost

This is a true story. I know it's not real, but it's the truth. Back in the eighties, if we were busy, we'd break up and go to lunch. I was always one of these persons that never ate breakfast. I never cared for breakfast back then. Therefore, I would go early to eat lunch. We were having a funeral this particular day, and there were several other things going on.

After I would go eat, there was a friend of mine that operated a business, and I'd stop to see him. If we had time, we would chat. Well, I stopped by to see him but had to park several businesses down the street from his. As I got out of my car, there was a gentleman standing in the doorway of a business. I spoke to him, totally sure in my head that that was Mr. So-and-So.

Today, all these years later, I am totally convinced that in my mind that was So-and-So. I spoke to him. In fact, I called him by his nickname. Then I went in and talked to my friend for ten or fifteen minutes, then got back in my car and came back to the funeral home. Well, this person I thought I had spoken to was lying on our table, getting ready to be prepared. He was found dead by his family on his sofa at his house in a totally different direction in the community from where I had seen him. There was no way possible that he could have been there when I saw him and spoke to him. But I will die always knowing that's who I spoke to, and he spoke back to me.

I don't know who it was I spoke to, but it wasn't the one who was found dead. However, in my mind, that's who I spoke to. You can imagine the shock of me coming back and finding him. I know that it was not him, and I know it wasn't a ghost. It was a human being standing there who called me by my name.

William Bledsoe, Irvine, September 26, 2007

NEED TO KEEP HOGS AWAY FROM BLOOD

I heard somebody tell a story one time about embalming. Back then, they'd take the blood out of the dead body and then bury the blood in some kind of container. I guess this is the truth, since this old man told me that it did happen. He said that hogs were out there where they buried the blood, and the hogs got into that blood, sucked it up, and it killed every one of them. [Laughter]

I don't know what the [dead] man died from, but they said the hogs all died. Evidently, they didn't bury the blood deep enough and the hogs got into it.

Bob Brown, Elizabethtown, September 25, 2007

FAINTER'S FALL

Late one afternoon, visitation was being held for a lady in our community. Her brother warned us that when his other sister arrived, we should be prepared for her to pass out when she saw her sister in the casket. So we got out the smelling salts and were waiting in the back of the room for the fall. To everyone's surprise, nothing happened and visitation went as planned.

The next day, we conducted the funeral service and went to the cemetery for burial, again without the sister fainting. The cemetery was across the road from the deceased woman's home. When the minister said his last amen at the grave site, everyone turned to leave and the action started.

The "fainting lady" came alive, or I guess you should say "out." She hit the ground before anyone could catch her and she was out cold. Her daughter straddled her and began shouting, "Momma, you can't die too!"

With that, the niece started running across the cemetery to her house shouting, "I'm going to call the ambulance," and I looked up to find my brother-in-law [a funeral director] chasing her and yelling, "We are the ambulance. We are the ambulance."

I could only stand back with the minister and laugh.

Ann Denton, Hardinsburg, November 9, 2007

Little Girl Wasn't Dead

When I was in school, Mr. Healman was one of the teachers. One day he was just giving us a list of some things we needed to do when we started our own funeral business. He said, "You get people in when you go pick them up, but don't put them on the table and then go out in the sitting room drinking coffee and smoking cigarettes. Be sure when you get them in there that everything is all right."

Some of the guys asked him, "Why?"

He said, "Because this is a true story, and I wouldn't tell you if it isn't true."

He then told us that these guys had a death call from the hospital, and they went and picked up this young girl and brought her to the funeral home and put her on the table. There were two or three guys sitting in there waiting, so when the others come back, they asked, "Where is she?"

"She's on the table."

Well, they were just sitting there talking to each other, and all of a sudden the little girl was standing in the door. One of the fellows looked around and said, "What did you say?"

Everybody looked at the same time and saw the little girl just standing there looking at them, and they couldn't believe what they were looking at, but it was her. She'd done got off that table and came in there. She wasn't dead!

They thought she was dead, but there she stood just looking at them. When she got off that table, she didn't know what it was all about. She just heard them talking, so she got off the table and walked in to see what they were doing. And there she stood in the door!

Someone asked them what they did after they saw her. They said they took her back to the hospital, then called her family and took her home. She wasn't dead!

The teacher then said to us, "Whenever somebody passes away, don't throw them on a table and then walk away, because they may not be dead."

But that won't happen in present times, because things are different now from the way they used to do things.

Ruby Taylor McFarland, Owensboro, December 17, 2007

The Clip-on Tie

We were having a viewing for a man an hour or so before the funeral service was to be held. Among the family members, there was some disagreement about what is called a clip-on tie. One of the grandchildren proceeded to go up to the casket and rip the clip-on tie off his grandpa and then run out the door.

Some family members ran after him, but I don't know whether they caught him or not. But when the eight pallbearers, who were all grandchildren, came up to view their grandfather for the last time, all of them took off their clip-on ties and placed them in the casket before we closed it.

Greg Woodruff, Salem, April 11, 2008

Buried Rings

I've had experiences relative to placing rings, jewelry, and stuff with family members. One particular case that I remember was to leave a ring on a lady, and it belonged to a blind granddaughter. When she took her ring off, she said, "Would you put this ring on Grandmother's hand?"

I placed the ring on her grandmother's finger. Then the blind granddaughter rubbed her hand over it and said, "Doesn't that ring look beautiful on Granny?"

I asked her if she would like to have the ring back, and she said, "I would."

Unfortunately, I didn't get the ring off, and it was buried with the body. I went back to the family the next morning after I realized the mistake I had made. I said to them, "I will be happy to disinter her, and I will get the ring up because the body was not placed in a vault."

I knew I could remove the casket and get the ring off, and the comment from the little blind girl was, "I feel like if you are that trustful to say that you will take her up, I know the ring is on her hand, and it looks better on her hand than it does on mine. So therefore, don't disturb the grave."

That was one sad experience that I had with burying jewelry.

I had this other experience too. There were two rings and three children. I was given specific instructions that each ring was to remain on their mother's hand. As I lowered the casket into the vault, one of the daughters grabbed me and said, "Where is Mother's rings?"

I said, "They are on her hands because I was instructed to leave the two rings on."

Well, they insisted that we get the rings off, so therefore I had to pursue the job to get the casket back to the top of the ground and raise it up. I started to open the casket, and it being a sealer-type casket, when I started to unseal the casket, the sealing mechanism broke. Thus, I couldn't get the lid open, and I knew it was sealed. They asked me, "How are you going to divide two rings between three children? If you feel the casket is sealed, put her back in the ground."

That was my other experience that I recall about making a mistake about buried jewelry out of my fifty years of professionalism. It looked like it worked out for the best, because I couldn't divide two rings between three children.

Charles Strode, Tompkinsville, May 29, 2008

Taking Body up a High Hill

I had a friend that used to work for a funeral home up in eastern Kentucky. I think it was Engle Funeral Home in Hazard. They were getting ready to have a funeral way out in the country in a country church. Billy Engle was owner of the funeral home, and Casey Compton was employed by Billy. Billy said to Casey, "Just go ahead and work that funeral by yourself."

Casey said that he got directions to the church and got out there. The church was setting up on a hill and was as steep as a cow's face and was rough. He stopped down there at the foot of the hill and saw this man standing up there. The man sort of yelled out, "Hit it hard and come on."

Casey said that he did, and that the casket fell out the back door, the dead body and all. The casket hit the ground, and there were women fainting everywhere. He said that it was a wooden casket and they finally got it. It was split on the bottom and had come apart some. Casey said, "I knowed that I was fired when I got back, and I told my boss. But the boss just laughed about it, and said, 'Ah, that's all right. Them things happen all the time.'" [Laughter]

It probably did happen a lot.

Billy Dowell, Mt. Vernon, August 27, 2007

New Hearse Passes Test

This took place in the 1970s. . . . We were needing another car hearse, and my boss was going to try out a beautiful black car that was, I believe, a 1971 Cadillac. A salesman brought by an S&S, which was one of the best-looking cars we ever had. Mr. Samples saw that car, and the minute I saw him looking at it, I knew that he was going to buy it, just by the look on his face.

He took it out for a test drive. Why he did it I don't know, for I don't know what you learn from a test drive. On the way back from the test drive, if you turn in to our driveway, especially at that time, you would kind of pull the car a foot or two to the left and swing into the driveway in order to comfortably turn in.

It just so happened that out in front of the funeral home there was no one parked in the parking spaces along the side of the street. So Mr. Samples did turn his turn signal on and was getting ready to come back in the car lot. Well, being curious, we were standing out there in the parking lot, watching him pull up. About that time, there was a brown car that went by, moving rather swiftly.

This lady who was driving that car, not paying any attention to what she was doing, saw that car getting ready to turn, and she just . . . went through the parking spaces to go by it. Mr. Samples didn't see her coming. Therefore he continued to make his turn, and she caught the front corner bumper of that big new Cadillac hearse. That was the worst wreck that you've ever heard.

She got stopped just a little beyond the post office, which is next to our funeral home. Of course, we took off running down to Main Street. Well, I'd have given anything if I had had a camera for you to see the look on Mr. Samples's face. He was a balding gentleman that sat very erect in the car and had both hands on the steering wheel. His head was turned, his mouth was wide open, and his eyes were as big as pears. He didn't know what in the hell hit him!

The amazing thing was, she hit the front bumper of her car and ripped it from her door clear back to the end of the car, wide open on the front bumper of that car, but never put a scratch on that new hearse. It did not put one scratch on it! But she hit that car just exactly right to catch the door. We couldn't find a mark on the hearse, but she tore her car all to pieces.

That was one of the funniest sights I believe I've ever seen in my entire life.

William Bledsoe, Irvine, September 26, 2007

CHURCH ON FIRE

Logan Dixon of Dixon-Atwood Funeral Home in Elizabethtown was having a funeral at Howell Valley Methodist Church one day, and it was wintertime and really cold. Somebody was driving down the road and noticed the church was on fire!

He stopped and went into the church, knowing the funeral was going on, and caught Mr. Dixon, who was in the back of the church. He said, "Hey, this church is on fire. You all had better get out of here."

They made the announcement the church was on fire, and the people started getting out. They got the casket and everybody out just barely before the church collapsed.

Bob Brown, Elizabethtown, September 25, 2007

WRONG COAT

We've got a friend who runs a funeral home in a surrounding community. They'd had a death call, and for some reason or another, I don't think the deceased person's family had brought in his clothes all at one time. Later on, they brought his suit coat in, and I think it was a blue pin-stripe coat or something pretty common.

The men that worked there at the funeral home had come in and asked the secretary if the family had brought the clothes in yet. Well, they had finished bringing them in, and the secretary says, "Yes, it's a blue suit hanging up in the office over there."

So they went and got the clothes and went up to the embalming room, dressed the body, and got it in a casket. They were getting ready to have the body out for visitation, but they were also going to have the funeral that same day for another person. When it got up closer to funeral time, the funeral home owner had gone into the office. When he came back out he asked, "Has anybody seen my suit coat?"

Well, come to find out, they had put his coat on the deceased person! [Heavy laughter]

I'm not sure how that ended up that day. I don't know whether he had to go through the funeral without a suit coat on or if he went home to change clothes real quick.

Bryson Price, Lewisburg, November 16, 2007

FUNERAL DIRECTOR'S PANTS FALL OFF

There was another funeral director, who weighed at least 350-plus pounds. His casket display room was upstairs in his funeral home. He was making arrangements with a family, and they got ready to select the casket. He started up the steps to lead them up there, and the farther he got up the steps, the lower his pants were coming down. By the time he got to the top of the steps, his pants fell completely down and he was standing there in nothing but his boxer shorts! [Heavy laughter]

That was an embarrassing moment for him. I'm sure the family got a big chuckle out of that. I suppose his pants fell all the way down to the ground before he could catch them.

Bryson Price, Lewisburg, November 16, 2007

WRONG DADDY

This is a story about a case of mistaken identity. This funeral home had a manager whose name was Casey Compton. He was one of them fellows that had a personality that I don't care what he did, you couldn't be mad at him. He could slap your dog and you wouldn't get mad at him. He just had that kind of personality! He was just a good funeral man, a good embalmer, and just a good mortician. He had a personality that everybody wished they had.

We were sitting in the funeral home, had a couple of visitations. This family came buzzing in there and went past all of us straight into the first chapel. Well, they commenced mourning all over the place, just crying and boo-hooing and hugging and kissing and consoling, just doing everything that a family grieving does. They just went on and on and on. And about that time, one of the fellows there at the funeral home said, "Casey, you know what family that is, don't you?"

Casey said, "Yeah, I do."

The other fellow said, "Casey, you know that ain't the right body they're mourning over, don't you?"

Casey said, "I do."

The fellow said, "Now, Casey, what are you going to do about that?"

Casey said, "Well, I'm just waiting for my opportunity to go up there and talk with them."

So, about that time, Casey sort of wandered up into the chapel there by the casket. One of the daughters come up and said, "Casey, I know you all do a good job, but I just don't think Daddy looks right. Daddy just don't look right. In fact, I don't even think that's the casket we picked out for Daddy, or the clothes"

Casey said, "Well, now honey, let me tell you what the problem here is. You see, that ain't your daddy. Your daddy is in the next room, if you want to go see your daddy."

Well, this was kind of embarrassing to the family, so Casey kind of put his arm around her and said, "Honey, you all just follow us over here." So he took them into the next chapel, and they commenced grieving and pondering and hollering and crying and helping each other through their grief.

Jay Steele, Pineville, January 20, 2008

Never Seen Him Dead Before

Another Casey story that I like to share is about this family that came in. He took them into the chapel, and they commenced mourning and crying and carrying on, just real emotional. This went on for a few minutes, and then they were just kind of complaining about everything: his hair wasn't right; his color wasn't right; the casket didn't match his shirt, and etc., etc. Nothing was right about Daddy. They just weren't happy at all. No matter what, they just weren't happy. Finally, the dead man's son turned around and said, "Casey, we're disappointed."

Casey said, "Well, why are you disappointed?"

The son said, "Well now, look at him. That don't look a thing like Daddy." He then went on about the other complaints.

Casey just stood there and never said a word. Finally, the son stopped complaining, and Casey said, "Let me tell you something, honey. I'm going to tell you exactly why your daddy doesn't look like himself."

They said, "What's that, Casey?"

Casey said, "Honey, you just ain't never seen your daddy dead before."

Well, that would have been something else I'd been slapped over if I had said something like that. The son stepped back there for a minute, looked at his daddy; looked at the rest of the family; looked back at Casey, and thought for a minute or two. You could tell he was a ponderer. Finally, he said, "Do you know what, Casey, you are exactly right. I just ain't never seen my daddy dead before, and when I get to thinking about that, he really don't look all that bad, and I'm sure that you all did the very best you could do. That's just the whole thing; I just ain't never seen my daddy dead before."

That's a true Casey story.

Jay Steele, Pineville, January 20, 2008

Brothers on the Dipsy Doodle Curve

Funeral homes were one of the first groups to actually supply ambulance service to communities, especially small and rural communities. . . . Back in the early days, the more red lights the ambulance had on it, the better the ambulance was.

This first ambulance story I want to share is about two brothers. One worked at a funeral home, and the other was a U. S. Marine recruiter. Two funeral homes were involved in this story, one of which is out of business now. For the sake of nonargument, I'm just going to call them Funeral Home A and Funeral Home B. They were called out to an accident, so Funeral Home A went flying out to the scene of the accident. The person wasn't hurt too bad, and they put him in the back of the ambulance and turned on all the red lights, because the more red lights they had, the better the ambulance was.

Coming back into town, there's a place there in the road called the Dipsy Doodle Curve. Well, as they were coming through that curve, the driver of the ambulance kind of lost control and ended up in the bottoms out there in the Dipsy Doodle Curve.

The young driver was kind of upset about this and didn't know what he was going to do, but fortunately nobody was hurt at all, other than the driver's pride. The patient in the back was okay, so they called Funeral Home A to send another ambulance out there. They loaded the patient up and left.

Well, that was going to be kind of an embarrassing circumstance for Funeral Home A and the driver. So his marine recruiting brother decided he was going to take care of his little brother. He got some marine recruiting stickers and put them all over the frosted glass in which the name of Funeral Home A was etched on the side of the ambulance.

So, this marine recruiter put these stickers all over the frosted glass to cover up the name of the funeral home. Then, when the news reporter got there and wanted to know who had the accident, the marine recruiter said, "Why, Funeral Home B come flying through here like there was no tomorrow and missed that curve and went plumb out into the bottoms. Funeral Home B ought to have known better than that."

It is a little weekly newspaper, so three or four days later the paper comes out, and sure enough there it is on the front page of the paper, "Funeral Home B has ambulance wreck in Dipsy Doodle Curve."

Now, *that's* a story about a brother covering a brother, and it is true.

Jay Steele, Pineville, January 20, 2008

On-Demand Oxygen

This is another story about Funeral Home A. That funeral home got a station wagon back when station wagons were cheaper than ambulances, cheaper than combinations, and cheaper than hearses. So funeral homes got to using station wagons when they got big enough to hold a cot. . . . Well, in a station wagon you couldn't quite put all the red lights on there, but you could put a real big red light on top. So, about 1970, we got a Buick station wagon, and we really liked that wagon because the tailgate would float all the way down under the car, and the window part would float up in the roof. So we didn't have to lean across the tailgate to get the cot in and out.

Well, it had a nice big red light on it, but the thing that impressed the heck out of all of us was that car had an on-demand oxygen mask. That just sounded right real impressive. We had the big red light, but we'd got an on-demand oxygen mask [too].

For about two weeks, we ran around there in town talking about this on-demand oxygen mask. Well, one day we were sitting in the office there at Funeral Home A, and one of the boys said, "You know, I've been thinking about this on-demand oxygen mask deal. On-demand means that they've got to be breathing to get that oxygen, don't it?"

We all concurred and agreed that that was right. Then he said, "You know, we're bragging about an on-demand oxygen mask, and he ain't breathing and he ain't getting no oxygen."

It didn't take us long to figure out that we needed to stop bragging about that on-demand oxygen mask but, man, we sure had a nice big red light on that car!

Jay Steele, Pineville, January 20, 2008

NOTIFICATION MISHAP

This is a story about a man who was killed in a car accident. At that time, funeral director A and funeral director B were serving their apprenticeships at XYZ Funeral Home. Funeral director A was kin to the man killed in the accident. Back at that time, not everybody had telephones and stuff up in the hollow, so they was trying to figure out how they was going to tell [the wife] that her husband died in a wreck.

They were sitting there talking, so the owner of the funeral home decided he was going to send his apprentices up there, because apprentice A was kin to the lady who was wife to the gentleman who died, and he could just tell her about the accident. And he sent apprentice B up there to kind of give them some moral support. So all the way up there, these apprentices talked about how they were going to tell her. Finally, B told A, "Now, you are going to tell her, not me. You are the one she is kin to."

They got up to the widow's house and knocked on the door. She came to the door, and she said, "Hello A and B, how are you all doing?"

"We're doing just fine, Mrs. C. How are you doing?"

She said, "Well, fine. Come on in."

Funeral Director A said, "Now, Mrs. C, I need to ask you a question."

She said, "Well, what's that?"

He said, "Did you want Mr. C embalmed?"

She said, "What do you mean, A?"

He said, "Well, he got killed in a car wreck awhile ago, and we just wanted to come up here to find out if you wanted him embalmed or not."

A says that is not a true story, but everybody that works at the funeral home says it *is* a true story. But that's how apprentice funeral director A told his next of kin how her husband, Mr. C, was killed in a car accident.

Jay Steele, Pineville, March 1, 2008

FUNERAL HOME REPUTATIONS

I started in this business in 1967. In Morgantown, there were two funeral homes, the Dwight Smith Mortuary, which was the oldest firm [1886], and the Ayers and Sharer Funeral Home that started in the early 1960s. There was a little store there in Morgantown named Renfrow's Market. There was also a black lady there in Morgantown, Miss Pearl Ratler, whom everybody knew and loved. On this certain day, she had been to a funeral that Mr. Ayers had in the Ayers and Sharer Funeral Home.

She was talking to Mr. Renfrow there at his store, and he said something to her about the funeral, and she said, "I'll tell you what, I always liked that Mr. Ayers, but I'm not going to have him to bury me. He ran them out of the cemetery. I know why he did that; he did that so when he takes the body out of the casket, he takes the casket back to the funeral home and resells it."

Mr. Renfrow looks at her and says, "Miss Pearl, I guess you'll have Smith Funeral Home to bury you."

She said, "Lord, no. They've been at it longer than he has!"

John A. Phelps, Bowling Green, March 3, 2008

BURIED ON A NINETY-FOOT BLUFF

In the funeral business, as serious as it is, if you don't find a little humor in it, I think we'd all [have] lost our minds. When James Pendley and I worked together, we both worked seven days a week, twenty-four hours a day. That means you might go for two or three weeks and not get a minute off. So, honestly, you'd have to find things to laugh at. If you didn't, I don't think any of us would have the mental capabilities for doing it.

Back in 1959 or '60, we were still in the old block building there in Brownsville that Charlie Townsend built in the 1940s. It had only one room for bodies, and if we had four bodies, we'd put them on four different walls. We didn't have funeral services at the funeral home back then. Everybody went to a church. This old building would snap and pop, and at three or four o'clock in the morning, if you were there by yourself when all that popping and cracking went on, it would make the hair on the back of your neck stand up.

We had a couple of communities, especially one area where they didn't have any phones. They had one radiophone in the whole community, and after about ten o'clock at night the ferry closed. So, most of the time when somebody over there died, the family would just wait until the ferry opened the next morning, and they'd come over to the funeral home to get us to come get somebody.

This particular area was a different area, but it was quite similar. One morning this guy walked up the steps, and he had a beard that he hadn't shaved in about two weeks. He was wearing an old hat, bib overalls, and an old flannel shirt. Don Sharer, who didn't know him, said, "Sir, could I help you?"

This fellow said, "Mister, I want to buy a coffin."

Don said, "Buy a coffin?"

He said, "Yes, sir, my mom died this morning, so I want to buy a coffin from you so I can take it home and bury my mom."

That wasn't really unusual at all, but Don did a pretty good job of mentioning that he'd be better off to let us bring the casket down there and a dress and bathe her and put her in a casket for him and everything.

"Oh, would you do that for me, sir?"

"Yes, sir, we'd be happy to do it."

"Well, I'd really appreciate it. What time are you all going to be there?"

Don told him; then the fellow said, "Well, I'll have my team and wagon waiting for you all at a certain location, because that would be as far as you could get in your truck."

Well, Don and Walter Reed—whom we often called "One Hair," because he didn't have a lot of hair and was a nervous fellow; he was the only guy I ever saw to go three or four directions at the same time, and he could always come up with something to cause you to laugh a little bit—they put the casket and the dress in this old panel truck and went forward. They took the body on the casket and dressed everything back there. And they took what instruments they needed to do the feature work and everything. So they went back there and bathed this old lady and put her in the casket. When he got done this fellow said, "We're going to have the funeral in the morning." He went on to tell what time it would take place, so Don convinced him to let him bring a tent down there and let his wife, Dolores, go with Walter to conduct the funeral. Then Walter come back down there and helped with the funeral, and Don was to go on to another service.

The funeral was that morning, but it was such a hard place to get to, we figured they wouldn't be back until way up in the evening. When we got out there to the cemetery, Dolores and Walter were the only two people there that could sing. Dolores always said that they must be doing a terrible job because they got everything placed in the cemetery, family seated, and what few neighbors were there. They started singing this song, sang the first verse, then started on the second verse when the fellow spoke up and said, "That's enough mister. We'll have the rest of the funeral in the springtime when the weather is better."

So, that was a short song for us. But the part of what happened that caused me to always remember the story most was this. Dolores was a Southern lady who was a wonderful person, but she was very, very gullible. You could walk her into about anything. So she just swore that this woman was buried right on the edge of a ninety-foot bluff. She said, "Jerry, they made us bury that old lady backwards. But just as sure as anything, when the Lord comes and she raises up from the grave, she's going to take one step and go right over that ninety-foot bluff." [Laughter]

Jerry B. Patton, Brownsville, March 3, 2008

One Size Fits All

In my early days, Don Sharer would leave for a day or two. When a leading person left, the funeral home always picks up business. We'd just get so busy we didn't know what we were doing. His wife was there at this particular time, and she didn't really trust me to wait on families. And looking back, I didn't really blame her.

She told me, "Maybe both of us can get by okay. You just stay in here with me and help me and we'll get by."

[For] this one funeral, we'd gotten all the information and we took the family back there to the selection room. They had selected the casket and everything was going pretty well.

This dead lady was a little odd-shaped, a little bit odd-sized. Her family had picked out this dress, and it was pretty. Due to the way they are pinned up, they look very narrow at that particular time. It didn't look like it would fit even a very small lady.

The family asked, "Are you sure this will fit Mom?"

Don's wife said, "Oh, yeah; they're adjustable."

Jerry B. Patton, Brownsville, March 3, 2008

WINGS FOR THE HEAVEN-BOUND

To be honest, the two outstanding funeral directors in our area were from two counties nearby. They were the two superior funeral directors of their day. One of them was really a great guy. This is a story about him.

He used to call me, and I'd go up there and help him quite a bit when he was busy. On a particular day, we'd done two or three funerals. Somebody came by and told me, said, "—— is a good guy."

I said, "Yeah, I think a lot of him. He is a tremendous guy, and I enjoy working with him. He can find a lot of humor in things."

This fellow said, "Well, we've got two other good funeral homes here in this county."

I said, "Well, you've got two pretty good places, but the fellow I mentioned is the only one up here that knows how to get your wings fitted on right. If you get buried by anybody besides him, you can't go to heaven. You'll just be up there flying in a circle, trying to get in!" [Laughter]

I did say that! It's one of my own.

Jerry B. Patton, Brownsville, March 3, 2008

FACE-SAVING MEASURE

This didn't happen to me, but this guy told me about it. . . . He kind of made a living out of funny stories about funeral directors. They had a big funeral, but I don't know what it was about. I guess we are a little bit more on the edge sometimes when we are dealing with a pretty tragic event. He said this was a tragic death, and when that happens it always elevates the crowd. In other words, there's a lot more people coming.

He said they were taking this casket to the grave, and like a lot of good funeral directors do, he was on one end of the casket that all the pallbearers were carrying and the other guy was on that one. He said for some unknown reason that he'll never know, he had his back to the grave and was walking backwards. . . . He said that all of a sudden, he fell in the grave. He didn't realize he was that close, but under he went!

Well, the pallbearers held up for just a second, but all of them were making a loud noise like sucking their breaths. He said, "Well, I couldn't think of anything else to say to save my dignity, so I just got up and helped myself go on, and told the pallbearers that we could go on now; it's six-foot deep." [Laughter]

Jerry B. Patton, Brownsville, March 3, 2008

PATIENT MISUNDERSTOOD

We had a fellow at home who had worked on riverboats, and he got sick. And he was actually working for my daddy as a butcher in the butcher store. He and Dwight Smith were really good friends, so this gentleman, Mr. Carson, came down to the funeral home and said, "Dwight, will you take me to Memphis? I want to go down there to the hospital."

At that particular time, that was the only Marine hospital anywhere close. There was also one at St. Louis, I think. Dwight took him down there and came on back, and a couple of days later, Mr. Carson was back in town. He came by the funeral home and Dwight was asking him questions. Dwight asked him, "What did they tell you?"

Carson said, "Well, they didn't tell me nothing, but they had a paper for me to fill out asking if something happened, who was going to take care of my remains. So I just got up and told them I'd take care of them, then just got up and left." [Laughter]

In his mind, he thought they were telling him he was going to die.

James M. Pendley, Morgantown, March 3, 2008

4

PERSONAL PRACTICE STORIES

∼

The following personal practice stories are about funeral events in which the funeral directors were personally involved and accountable. They are oral history accounts in which the storytellers experienced what took place, whether good or bad. By sharing their stories with other funeral directors, employees, and the general public, they are letting the world know about the wonderful ups and downs of the funeral service profession.

The stories involve embalmings, grave site selection, suicides, homicides, and military funeral services. Some mention snake handling, bedbugs, and animals in the funeral home. Others give accounts of apprenticeships, of driving ambulances and hearses, and of breaking up family fights. All provide information and insights about managing a funeral business and interacting with bereaved families and community members.

NOTES ON CROW'S FUNERAL HOME SERVICES

Years ago, some people in furniture and general store businesses made certain kinds of furniture and also provided caskets that they also made, which were called coffins in the old days. The Crow's Funeral Home service probably stemmed from that kind of business.

Up until the 1950s, most of the funeral directors would go to the homes to do the embalming, dress the body, bring the casket to the house, and sometimes have the visitation there at the home, [with] the funeral at church or sometimes in the front yard. They built our main chapel in the 1950s that we have now. When that happened, it was a big addition in terms of cultural changes. People started using the chapel here for funerals more often than we did in churches. However, we still use churches for funerals quite often. And we started having more funerals here at this funeral home because we had a nice chapel that was probably bigger than most churches.

The practice of keeping the body at home for viewing and for funeral services has not stopped completely. Once every few years we'll take a body home like they used to do. But that's very seldom done anymore.

When I started working here by myself in August 1971, doing my apprenticeship, I was eighteen years old. At that time we would still take a few people home each year, back in the early seventies. We might take four or five home each year for visitation purposes. Then when it was time to bury the body, we would go back to the house to take the body to the cemetery. Generally, we would go from the home to a church for a funeral, then from the church to the cemetery, as is traditionally done now.

When we would take the body to the home for the viewing and visitation, we didn't always stay there, but we would go back periodically to check to see that everything was okay and to see if they needed anything. Of course, when we did that, we would also take over chairs and sometimes fans when people didn't have the ability to cool their homes.

We also took along a boxed set of portable curtains. We would take that box into the home, then find a corner in the living room, then unfold and open the box. The curtains would unfold out of that box and telescope up to where it looked like a backdrop for the casket. The curtains were usually velvet, maroon or dark-colored velvet material that had a swooping design on the front. The curtains would be a backdrop for the casket. We also put lamps at the head and foot of the casket to give the desired lighting effect over the open casket.

Of course we had casket stands, or what in more recent times are called church trucks. The old name for them was "catafalque," that the casket would be placed on. It was also called a casket bier. That was actually a casket stand on which the casket is placed during visitation or viewing. Presently, we call it a church truck; at least, we call it that around here. It is a portable, collapsible, four-wheel truck that we can put the casket on and roll it in and out of the church.

Follis Crow, Glasgow, December 11, 2007

Wait till She Dies

When Martin and I first bought this funeral home, we did ambulance service up until 1972. One Sunday afternoon, we got an ambulance call to come out to the Red Hill section and bring this lady to the hospital. I took the call myself and went out there. At that time, I was by myself.

This lady was there in the hospital bed, and she was in terrible shape. One of her daughters said to me, "Billy, do you think she's dying?"

I said, "Yes, I do."

She said, "Well, just sit down over there and wait till she dies. Then take her on to the funeral home." [Laughter]

In about fifteen or twenty minutes she died, so I brought her to the funeral home.

Billy Dowell, Mt. Vernon, August 27, 2007

Bad Enough Heart Attack

I'm a coroner here in the county and have been for quite a while. I received a coroner call about an elderly person, suddenly and unexpected. We got the body, and the family was there the next day to make funeral arrangements. One member of the family said, "Mr. Dowell, what do you think killed Paul?"

I said, "Well, from everything you told me about all the symptoms, he had a heart attack."

The fellow asked me, "Was it a ba-a-ad one?" [Heavy laughter]

It's kind of hard not to smile sometimes!

Billy Dowell, Mt. Vernon, August 27, 2007

Family Gravedigger

Five or six years ago I was piddling around over here at my daughter's house doing something. Steve Martin [Roy Martin's son] came over there and said to me, "Billy, you'd better come over to the funeral home; come over there pretty quick."

I said, "What's going on?"

He said, "Come on over."

He was kind of shook up, so I go. When I got there, this man was setting there in his car, and his wife was over here in the passenger seat, dead.

So, I was talking to this man and asked him, "What happened, Lester?"

He said, "Well, she got up this morning; she fixed my breakfast and I ate it. She said, 'I think I'll go back here and lay down,' and she did. And she took bad, and I was going to take her to the hospital, and she died. I already had her in the car when she died. I thought, well, there ain't no use taking her back to the house, so I'll just take her to the funeral home. It's the coroner's place, so I'll just deliver her up there."

I asked him, "Well, what do you want to do, Lester?"

He said, "Nothing."

I said, "Do you want her embalmed?"

He said, "No, they ain't no use of that. I'll go down here to pick out a casket, and you bring her down to the cemetery tomorrow and we'll bury her."

I said, "You don't want her laid out?"

"No, there's not much point in it."

So that's what we did. We dressed her and put her in a casket. Lester left the funeral home and didn't come back to the funeral home. But he dug the grave himself.

He also dug the grave for his parents, too, by himself. Then he put the soil back in the grave on top of the casket.

It rained a flood that day while we were at the cemetery. He had a tarpaulin stretched over the grave so he wouldn't get rained on while he was digging, but he still got soaking wet from that blowing rain.

Billy Dowell, Mt. Vernon, August 27, 2007

AFRAID TO TOUCH THE DEAD

We had a death call down on Trace Branch, which is out of Livingston, in the middle of the night. I went by myself down there to pick the body up. I figured there would be quite a few persons there as the person had been on their deathbed for quite a while. When I got there, the first man I saw was Bill Coles. Bill was a good fellow, and I was going to get him to help me, so I said, "Boy, Bill, I am glad to see you. I need some help picking Mr. —— up."

He said, "Lord God, honey, I love you, but I wouldn't touch him for a million dollars." And he wouldn't. He was terribly afraid of any dead body, so he wouldn't even drive by a cemetery after dark!

Billy Dowell, Mt. Vernon, August 27, 2007

Spend Every Bit

There was a sad case involving this man who died of cancer. He had a substantial insurance policy back at that time. I think it was ten thousand dollars. His widow came in to make arrangements and said, "Now, I want to spend every bit of that insurance on Ed."

I told her, "You've got to go on living, too. You're going to need some money."

"I don't want it," she said. "He worked for it, he paid for it, and I'm going to spend every bit of it on him."

And she did. She bought the best things we had. She even had us purchase a copper vault for him. So, she spent every bit of that insurance money on him. Her request was that she wanted to be the last one out of the funeral home. She followed his casket out.

I don't remember who sang the song during the time as we left the chapel, but it was a country music singer that sang "There Goes My Everything." And she didn't live a lot longer after that, as grief may have had something to do with it.

Billy Dowell, Mt. Vernon, August 27, 2007

Man Shoots Himself

I was getting ready to leave the funeral home back a few years ago. My telephone rang, and it was a man from over in the Eubank section of Pulaski County. He told me who he was and said, "Why don't you come out? I want to talk to you about funerals."

I said, "Well, it's kind of late. Would it be all right to come out in the morning?"

"Nope, it will be too late then."

I said, "Well, all right. Tell me how to get there."

So, he gave me directions, and I got in a car to drive out there. It was a farmhouse that sat probably one hundred yards off the road. I drove up to his house on the driveway, got out, knocked on the door, and his wife came to the door. In a rough voice she said, "Who are you and what do you want?"

I said, "Well, I'm Billy Dowell. Sam called me a while ago and wanted me to come out here."

"Well, he's in there. Go on in."

I went in, and he was in his bed. He got up on all fours and looked around. He was wild looking. He was seeing tanks and armored vehicles coming up the highway. He finally calmed down a little bit and said, "Do you know what Social Security pays? What VA pays, and any other help?"

I tried to explain to him the best I could. Then he said, "What I'm going to do, I'm going to kill myself tonight."

Naturally I tried to talk him out of it. But he said, "You can't talk me out of it. The government has killed me. It has done me in, so I'm going to kill myself with that gun right there."

There was a .410 shotgun hanging over his bed. His wife had been in there listening to all of this. So, I stayed out there, I guess two hours, talking to him, trying to talk him out of it. But I didn't, and that night he stuck that shotgun in his mouth and killed himself. The gun blew his head off. And I don't doubt that his wife handed him the gun.

He was suffering, though, for he had cancer that had gone to his brain. But he blowed his head off with that shotgun. That happened several years ago.

Billy Dowell, Mt. Vernon, August 27, 2007

GRIEVING OVER WIFE

A man in his late sixties lost his wife after a short illness. I picked the body up and asked the husband if he could come to the funeral home that afternoon to make arrangements. He did not have an automobile and couldn't drive. A neighbor gentleman brought him to the funeral home to finalize arrangements. While there, he talked on and on about his wife and what a hard worker she was. She could strip more tobacco, hoe more corn, and chop more wood than most men. Then he would cry and wail. His driver told him, "Now, O. P., get a hold on it. I lost my wife three years ago and I've made it just fine."

O. P. looked at the man and replied, "Yes-s-s, brother, but you can cook."

Billy Dowell, Mt. Vernon, August 27, 2007

CASKETS ON WHEELS

When funerals first started, as I can remember, funeral workers would go to homes to embalm the bodies. Then they'd lay the body out on a rug in the house. Sometimes these old houses were kind of collapsed, kind of worn out. Sometimes the floor would be leaning, swaying. We always embalmed the body in the bedroom. We had equipment that was gravity flow. It was in bottles that we would hang up high as we could in the ceiling, then let that fluid run down into the body. That fluid would cause the body to last pretty good for two days.

Back then, we used church trucks that were sometimes called biers. These are the tables or racks that you see the casket setting on when you go to the funeral home for visitations or funerals. They are tables with wheels on them that roll the casketed remains around.

I remember times when, in preparing for funerals, we had to use trucks that had wheels on so as to roll caskets to the house. Sometimes we'd have to prop the casket so it wouldn't roll down toward the family when they were sitting in there.

If they rolled down toward the family, that would bother them. But we'd prop the casket good so it wouldn't do that. If the casket started rolling, it would scare the family members. We sure didn't want that.

Edward Dermitt, Leitchfield, August 29, 2007

FIVE BROTHERS KILLED

I remember one occasion when five brothers were all killed at the same time.

They had a car wreck in Brandenburg. So family members wanted them all fixed to look at. We called in all the funeral directors we could get around to help us to prepare these bodies and get them ready.

I personally helped prepare the bodies and get everything ready. Then, me being a minister, all of their family members wanted me to preach the funeral. We had two funeral chapels and just opened up doors to both of them. We fixed it so people could march in and march out.

That happened thirty-five years ago. The brothers had motorcycles in the back end of a car, and they run over a cliff and that killed them all. It tore the car and motorcycles all to pieces.

I never will forget that a lawyer said, "Well, you are making a record here. This kind of thing has never happened in Leitchfield nor in Grayson County." He also said, "We've never had a Catholic and Baptist to work together [to preach a funeral]."

Edward Dermitt, Leitchfield, August 29, 2007

PREACHER SAVES THE DAY

Sometimes oversights can be made. After all, we are human. Mother had taken the flower car and went to the church. Dad and I were to follow. Dad and I were riding along in the hearse, taking the body to the church for the funeral. A funeral procession is to be lined up first by the preacher, then the hearse, then the next of kin, and so forth.

As we were riding along, Dad looked at me with a panic in his eyes. I exclaimed and asked him, "What is it?"

Dad turned pale, then barely in a whisper said, "We forgot the church trucks." The church truck is a bier, or the device on which the casket sets at the church, and it has wheels.

"Oh, no! What do we do?" I asked him, feeling a lump forming in my throat. We sat there in silence for a few seconds that seemed to be an eternity. "Give me the keys to the funeral home," I said. Dad complied.

Next came the dilemma of how I was going to get back to town. "Uh, we'll have to get the preacher to take me back," I said, as my heart began to race. I'm sure it was going faster than the funeral procession. Then, without another word and before I knew what was happening, Dad started passing the preacher's car! Here we are in the funeral procession in the hearse, carrying the beloved corpse and picking up speed in the momentum of pulling alongside the preacher.

Bless his heart, the preacher looked out the window to his left and saw the hearse and me waving at him to pull over. His eyes got as big as quarters! I can only imagine what was going through his mind.

We all stopped. I ran around to jump in his car, but the door of his car wouldn't open. The handle was broken. I couldn't get in. The procession was still creeping along and I didn't want it to have to come to a complete stop for me! For crying out loud, I was in a full-fledged panic. He had to reach over and open the door. I told him of our dilemma, and we turned around and went back to the funeral home to fetch the trucks.

By the time the preacher and I reached the church, the flowers were unloaded, the hearse parked, with pallbearers lined at the back. The church was packed and waiting for the preacher and me. Brother Danny slammed it into park and we jumped out. I pulled the trucks from his trunk and ran to the church. Just as I opened them, the pallbearers were entering with the casket.

Whew! That was too close for comfort.

Connie Hughes Goodman, Fountain Run, September 11, 2007

GROWING UP

As a child, I grew up living beside the family funeral home. My grandparents lived in the funeral home. I was allowed to play anywhere on the grounds except the "prep" room [morgue]. My experience growing up around the funeral home is one that did not affect my mental capacity or make me scared of the dead. In fact, I have fond memories of meeting lots of friends. I played with children who had relatives at the funeral home. Some I saw again and some I did not. I consider it a blessing to have come in contact with so many different wonderful people. I would say that this diverse experience contributed to my outgoing personality.

Life in the funeral business is not easy. You are on call twenty-four hours a day, seven days a week, and 365 days a year. When I was very small, I resented the fact that I had to stay with babysitters while my parents worked on the weekends. But as I grew up and am now a funeral director myself, I see that we have an obligation to our community. But understand, if the phone rang during a holiday meal, it usually meant that our family gathering was cut short. I can remember different times that we'd be eating or having fun. The phone would ring and everyone would stop in his/her tracks, fearful that it was a death call.

Connie Hughes Goodman, Fountain Run, September 11, 2007

BODY OIL

When I was twelve or so years old, I can remember going with Dad to the graveyard. In earlier years, Dad hired men to did graves by hand, but later he bought a small Bobcat. It had rained all night, and Dad said that he needed me to go with him to bail the water out of the grave. So I went.

I remember Dad handing me a bucket with a rope tied to it. He just told me to start dipping the water out of the grave. I began my task, but it simply baffled me about the iridescent oily film that floated on top of the water. I inquired about it, and Dad told me that it was oil from the decomposing body in the next grave.

With each bucketful of water, I contemplated that I was throwing a part of that other body out upon the ground. But I was only throwing his oil.

Connie Hughes Goodman, Fountain Run, September 11, 2007

SAME SONG FOR HUSBAND AND WIFE

We had a funeral a few years ago after this gentleman died who was from Muhlenberg County. It was a morning funeral, and my boss at the time was going to take the body back after the service to Muhlenberg to be buried.

The service was over about eleven thirty, and I went to my car about the time the procession was pulling out. The radio happened to be on. I think it was John Prine singing on the radio "Take Me Back to Muhlenberg County."

I know this is going to be hard to believe, but several years later this man's widow died. Same routine: I went to my car after the morning service and turned the radio on, and that same song was being played over the radio!

William Bledsoe, Irvine, September 26, 2007

SHAFTED BY MOTHER AND SON

This lady had a son who was very bad about paying bills, and my boss had had expericncc with him. A situation occurred where he had to have dealings with him again.

This fellow's mother came in and asked my boss if she signed a note, would he take care of the situation her boy was in. Actually, my boss was a very compassionate person and probably knew he wasn't going to get paid that time. But it represented a movement forward, so he went along with it. The note was due to be paid in six months. Six months then came up, and I was sitting in the office. I guess he was a little upset: "Well, I've been taken again."

So, he called her and told her the note was due. She asked him what that meant, and he said, "Well, it means that you owe the note. You signed it and he hasn't paid it."

She said, "But I didn't sign that note to pay it. I signed that note so you'd let him have what he wanted."

Again, [my boss], the same person who [drove] the hearse, with the bald head and the very erect body, his face turned crimson red, and I wondered what in the world is wrong with him.

Every once in a while, a young person who is not real smart and is *not* the boss takes directions from the boss and becomes smarter than the boss! He hangs the phone up, actually slams it, [and] says, "I'm going to take her to court." At that moment, I was smarter than this man whose intelligence I have never questioned. I said to him, "You're going to make a fool out of yourself."

He said, "What do you mean?"

I said, "Stop and think about it. You are going over to Small Claims Court. You are going to present that bill to court, and that little old lady is going to stand there in front of that judge and say, 'But Judge, he made me sign that, [but] I didn't sign it to pay it. I signed it so my son could get what he wanted.' And they're going to laugh you out of that court." [Laughter]

He took my advice. There are several things you can get out of that. Every once in a while, no matter how smart you are and how much experience you've had, there will be some little guy sitting around that can give you some of the best advice you've ever had, and you had better listen to it, especially when your emotions get into it. Also, there's a fine line between compassion and having the shaft stuck to you several times. And that's what he was into. He had been shafted by this one person several times, and yet he had this compassion for people in this situation, and that got him into that.

William Bledsoe, Irvine, September 26, 2007

MEDICARE QUESTION

I hadn't been in the funeral business very long when we had an ambulance run. I was very inexperienced. Mr. Huckleberry, who was one of the co-operators in this funeral home at the time, was the son-in-law of Mr. Lewis. He called me and said, "Will you meet me at the funeral home? We have an ambulance run."

It was getting about dusky dark when we pulled up in front of this house. This little fellow comes out. I vaguely knew who he was. But as we pulled up there in the ambulance, I noticed that Mr. Huckleberry didn't get out of the car [hearse], so I just set in the car with him. It was very unusual to go on an ambulance run and not get out of the car.

This comes under the heading of "What you don't know, you will find out." So, I set there waiting for Ed to get out, and this little gentleman walks out of the house and comes clambering up this little grade and walks around the car and opens the back door to the ambulance. He [gets] into the ambulance, sets down in the jump seat, and closes the door. That's our patient!

Well, just before he seated himself, he said, "Mr. Huckleberry, will it pay my—?" And that's as far as he got. And Ed said, "No, it won't." Not another word was said.

I thought, that's a strange conversation. Well, Ed put the car in reverse, started to back it around, turn around, and head back to the hospital with him.

This fellow said, "Wait just a minute, Mr. Huckleberry. The girls are coming with my purple Kool-Aid."

So these girls come up the hill and hand this quart canning jar with Reynolds Wrap on the top of it, a rubber band around it, and in it is grape Kool-Aid. So they gave him this jar of grape Kool-Aid to take with him. Mr. Huckleberry drives on up to the hospital and parks. [The gentleman] gets out with this grape Kool-Aid, walks on into the emergency room. When we got through with whatever we were doing, we get back in the car, and I said, "Ed, I'm totally lost."

He said, "Well, what is it Woody?"

First of all, I said, "Mr. So-and-So got up and he got in the car, and we didn't get out or anything."

He said, "Oh, I'm always used to coming out here and he always walks out. Nothing wrong with him."

I said, "Okay, when he got into the car, he asked you a question, and you just stopped him right in the middle of it and answered him."

He said, "Oh, he always asks me the same question."

I said, "Well, what is that question?"

He said, "He asks, 'Will my Medicare card pay for it?'"

Well, Ed had heard that question so many times he knew what he was going to ask. So, before this fellow finished asking the question, Ed said, "No, it won't."

Of course, I went on to get to know this fellow quite well myself. He always asked me the same question. We'd go out once every two months or so to get him; same question. [And] it was either purple Kool-Aid or green Kool-Aid.

William Bledsoe, Irvine, September 26, 2007

JUST WAIT

I had gone out on an ambulance run in my early twenties. I don't remember whether it was a shooting, a fight, or somebody that got hurt in a car wreck. Whatever the results of the whole thing were, I came back in and said to Mr. Huckleberry, "Ben, I have seen it all."

He said, "No, you haven't."

Guess what. He was right and I was wrong. You have never seen it all!

William Bledsoe, Irvine, September 26, 2007

FUNERAL PROCESSION MISSES THE EXIT

This story is about a funeral procession. Brother Billy Compton, who is pastor of Severns Valley Church, and I were going together to Louisville Memorial Gardens to have a graveside service. We had ten or so cars behind us going up I-65. We went to Watterson Expressway and turned left on it to get over to Shively.

We were having a good time talking, so when we got up there to Watterson, we missed a turn. We were supposed to get onto Watterson, but we missed it. Brother Billy said, "We missed that turn!"

I said, "Yeah, I know."

Then he said, "What are we going to do?"

I said, "Well, we'll just go to the next exit, which is the fairgrounds exit, and we'll take that exit."

So that's what we did. We pulled right up in front of the fairgrounds, and I knew we had to make a left turn to get back on Watterson Expressway. And believe it or not, there was a policeman setting across the road, and he's watching us. One of the sons-in-law of the man that died said, "Hold on, Brother Compton. I want to address something to Mr. Brown."

Brother Compton said, "You've got the floor."

Then this fellow said, "Mr. Brown, I want to know something. Do you charge for your service by the mile?" [Laughter]

I said, "Yes, I do, but I won't charge you any extra today!"

That kind of broke the ice and everybody laughed. Then we went right along.

We've had some other experiences, but that was likely the funniest experience I've ever had. I've heard of another person doing the same thing once. They had to take a funeral procession through McDonald's drive-in to get it turned around and go back in the right direction. Glad that wasn't me!

Bob Brown, Elizabethtown, September 25, 2007

LADY FAKED A FAINT

We used to have a lady that went to funerals all the time. She was here just about every time we had a funeral. Every time she went to a funeral, whenever we passed the crowd around by the casket she would pass out every time. In most cases she wasn't a part of the family, but she would walk by the casket and look in, carry on, and pass out right in the middle of the floor. And sometimes we thought it was a sort of put-on.

We saw her doing [it] so much that we'd be there somewhere pretty close and try to catch her to keep her from hitting the floor.

Anyway, she just continued doing it, and we just got tired of that. One day we said, "Well, we're just going to let So-and-So hit the floor this time." We did; we let her hit the floor. She didn't break any bones, but that was the last time she ever did that!

Bob Brown, Elizabethtown, September 25, 2007

FAMILIES NOT CLOSE ANYMORE

It has got so that people who come in here are not close to each other. Families are not close anymore. They're not close, and when you start asking them questions about their family, they don't even know their mother's maiden name, and stuff like that. Then you ask them if they have a minister, and after thinking about it, they'll say, "No. Don't you have somebody you can get?"

I'll say, "I know a lot of preachers, so you tell me what religion, and we'll go from there."

Sometimes they can't even think of anybody. They'll say, "Well, So-and-So got married not too long ago. Who was that preacher that preached the marriage ceremony?"

That kind of thing happens all the time. It's not at all uncommon. So it's up to me to call whatever preacher they want.

Sometimes I wonder why they even have a funeral.

We had a funeral just about a week ago, and the man that headed the funeral didn't know this man at all. They weren't church people, didn't go to church hardly ever. They had the funeral but it lasted only about twenty minutes. And they had moved the casket from the front of the chapel to the back of the chapel to let people file by.

They got about half of that crowd out, and all at once the brother of this man that died stood up and made a big spiel. He said, "I've got to say something." Then he starts reminiscing about things that were very inappropriate at that time. It might have been appropriate if he had been a part of the service, [but] half the people were already out of the chapel.

Everybody on the outside had heard it, and they asked, "What's going on in there?" That happened within the last two weeks.

Bob Brown, Elizabethtown, September 25, 2007

THE DEAD LOOK YOUNGER

Sometimes people come in and look at a body and when they see it, they think we've brought the dead person back and made them look twenty years younger. We've got a woman's body in here right now, and family members said that her lips are too big. They've been used to seeing her in a fetal position and she had no teeth. No wonder that her lips look bigger [since we put in some teeth]. The embalming process also fills out the lips, too.

So we didn't put any more makeup on than we had to, because she wasn't used to wearing makeup. But the first thing they said was, "Her lips are too big."

We didn't do anything else, because there's nothing you can really do. But what we do makes you look younger for one thing. It just makes you look different. Your lips are not going to look the same! [Laughter]

Things like that do happen sometimes, but most people are pretty easy to get along with. They're pretty satisfied with what they see, because we've improved it.

Bob Brown, Elizabethtown, September 25, 2007

ILLEGAL PURSUIT OF BURIAL SITE

We had this man that died who was from Glendale. His family came in to make arrangements. His wife said, "I want the funeral held at Gilead Baptist Church, which is in Glendale, down by the orphans' home, and I want him taken to Cave City for the burial."

I said, "Well, we can handle that."

Well, the mayor of Cave City is a funeral director. His name is Bob Hunt. I asked her where the grave was, and she told me it would be in the cemetery. I called Bob Hunt to see if he could dig the grave. He said, "Yeah, I can do that. I'll take care of that."

We left Glendale and headed for Cave City. We got down there and pulled into the cemetery. It just so happened Bob was right there, and he said, "We've got a problem. There's already a body buried in that grave that you wanted opened. Even the gravedigger didn't even notice it. They came from Bowling Green to put the vault in the ground, and the guy that was on the vault truck knew exactly what he was seeing. He looked down at the bottom of that grave and there these bones are. There's not a stone up here. No stone was found."

He told us, "We can't put him in that grave because there's already another body there."

So I said, "Well, we'll go on and have the funeral service, but after that we won't bury him. I'll gather the family together and see what they have to say about it."

So when the service was over, I told the family that we needed to have a little talk. So, we got the wife and the kids all together. I said to the widow, "Did you know there's already a grave where you told me to put your husband?"

She said, "Oh yeah, I moved the stone several years ago."

I said, "What?! You moved the stone but you didn't move the body?"

She said, "No, I just moved the stone so we could bury my husband there."

I said, "Well, we can't do that. We can't bury him in that grave." And the kids all said, "Well, Mother, you can't do that."

I said to her, "I don't know what you're going to do, but I'm going to take him back to E-town. You all are going to have to decide what you want to do."

They said, "Well, we'll call you back in the morning."

I said, "Okay, let me know." I came back to E-town, made the circle back here, pulled into the parking lot, backed up to the back door. I walked in and told everybody, "I need a little help out here to unload this body."

"You didn't go after a body. What are you talking about?"

I said, "Well, I brought the one back I was supposed to bury." [Laughter] Of course, I had to explain to them what was going on. But that was funny.

The next morning the kids went down to Glendale Christian Church, and there's a big cemetery there. That's where they wanted to bury their daddy in the first place. They got their way in the end, and that's where they buried him.

All they did down at Cave City was just fill the grave back up.

So the kids got their way after all. They said, "This is where Daddy wanted to be buried. I don't know why our mother wanted him way down there in Cave City."

Of course, she was a native of Cave City. That's the reason. She said, "I moved that stone several years ago!" That was a classic situation.

Bob Brown, Elizabethtown, September 25, 2007

CASKET EMPTIES ELEVATOR

If you want to ride in an elevator in the hospital, take a casket with you. We had a situation when a woman was in the hospital and her husband died. She was so sick and had so many tubes running out of her, she couldn't leave the hospital. This was the old St. Anthony Hospital in Louisville. It's now another hospital across from the old Baptist Hospital.

They have a beautiful chapel in St. Anthony, decorated with imported Italian marble and stuff. It's an old Catholic hospital. So, this widow wanted us to bring her husband up there in a casket so she could see him and have a little brief service there in the hospital. The hospital approved it and all that was needed.

My son was about fifteen or sixteen at that time, and he went with me. So we took the casket in and had pushed the elevator button to go up to the right floor. But there was somebody on that elevator, and when they saw we had a casket there, they just got out of the elevator and said, "Here, you go before us."

So, if you want an elevator at the hospital, just take a casket with you! They'll let you have the elevator. [Heavy laughter]

Terry Dabney, Campbellsville, October 13, 2007

WRONG TERRY

One of the funniest things that ever happened to me was when this guy was here as a corpse. His name was Terry, the same as mine. I had an older lady working with me, and somebody came in and said, "Is Terry here?"

I was upstairs, and this lady said to him, "Why sure. Come here and I'll show you where he is."

Well, she brought him up here to see me, but [he was] wanting to see the corpse!

I thought that was funny.

Terry Dabney, Campbellsville, October 13, 2007

REWARDED WITH FOOD

Of course, back years ago everybody took their family bodies home from the funeral home. One of my first recollections about helping my daddy here was that years and years ago nobody used a funeral home for their visitation. The bodies were always taken home, and you would take your chairs, take your register stand, take your lamps, and things like that.

My father had a fellow by the name of Bill McCrocklin that worked for him. Bill's job was to always go to the house, after my father had gone to the church for the funeral, to pick up and get all these things out while the funeral was going on.

So Daddy let me go a few times with Bill, and I soon found out why he always wanted to do that. And I soon found out that I wanted to go too, because when we were out there gathering all these things up and putting them in the vehicle to bring back here to the funeral home, there was always a bunch of women that would be there at the house preparing a meal for the family. As soon as we got through with our work, they'd say, "Well, Mr. McCrocklin, would you and Field like to have something to eat?"

Well, it didn't take me but one time to find out that was the kind of job I wanted to do because we always got country ham, or mashed potatoes, and other things, and we always got to eat before the family did, because we were getting everything out. So that was a fond memory that I have as a little boy.

Rayfield Houghlin, Bloomfield, October 17, 2007

FLOWER BOY

Before vans became popular, they used to load the flowers in an ambulance, [but] not the kind of ambulance that they have now. The ambulance I'm talking about [is like] the old hearses and things like that. They'd call them a combination.

I was small enough that when they brought the flowers out, I could stand up in the ambulance and load those flowers. Nobody else could load them but me because I was short enough and little enough. I didn't have to bend over; I'd walk back there to the back door, then walk back up to the front. That was my job; I'd load the flowers. These flowers were purchased, not homegrown. They were purchased from the flower shop here in Bloomfield, and they were the ones you always transported to the cemetery.

I can remember doing that as a child. That was my job. Of course, I wasn't old enough to drive. I'd get up in there and ride out to the cemetery. Then I'd crawl back up in that ambulance and carry the flowers to the back door. They'd carry them over to the grave and set all of them up. I was the flower boy!

Rayfield Houghlin, Bloomfield, October 17, 2007

LACK OF PERSONAL TIME

As a funeral director, your schedule is never your own. You are always on somebody else's time. It's one of those situations where you are always at the mercy of the people and the ringing of a phone. I've made plans to take my children somewhere and would have to cancel. I can remember one morning we were making plans to go to Gatlinburg and I got a death call. Well, when you're the only funeral director in town, it's hard to take off and leave.

Now, I have some more help, so if I feel like I want to take off and go somewhere, I feel comfortable in doing that

Rayfield Houghlin, Bloomfield, October 17, 2007

Second in the Food Line

There is a black church about four miles down the road, and the minister always rides to the cemetery with me after we have the funeral down at the church. The people always have a wonderful meal at the church. . . . The minister always tells me, "Now, Mr. Houghlin, you get with me, 'cause after I've blessed the food I always say, 'Now, ministers and morticians go through the line first, followed by the immediate family.'"

I'm always grateful to the minister down there, because he always goes first and I always get to go second! That's always been something that's stuck in my mind. I always look forward to having the funeral because I know I'll always be the second one to eat when I go down there! [Laughter]

Rayfield Houghlin, Bloomfield, October 17, 2007

Unforgettable Experience

I got a call one night from a person who lived six or eight miles out in the country. I called and asked an employee to go there with me. . . . We arrived at this very modest home, and when we went in, the husband of the lady who was deceased said, "No, she can't go to your place for preparation. I want it done here."

We tried to convince him that it was going to be very difficult to do it in a small house that would be crowded. But he said, "Absolutely not."

Well, we had to come all the way back to town to get all of our equipment. We went back out there, then had a very difficult time in preparing the body. She was in a terrible condition to begin with, but we finally got it done.

The next day or so, we took a casket out to that home. In order to get in the house, we had to remove a window. There was only one room we could have possibly got into with a casket. Finally, we got her placed in the casket, and that room was where we had to hold the funeral service. They said they were going to have prayer and a short service before we went to a church.

I stood by the casket when they were ready to do the service, and people jammed into the room. The service began with two songs and about thirty-five minutes of preaching. So there I stood by the casket, and it was ninety-degree weather.

That's my one experience I will never forget, and I hope I'll never go through one like it again!

William Lee Shannon, Shelbyville, October 25, 2007

SEEING THE BODY

The government shipped military veterans back during wartimes, and a lot of times they were in sealed caskets with instructions not to open them. That created a rather difficult situation with next of kin that wanted to see that person. Sometimes we would compromise a little bit by asking the family, "Would you allow us to look first, so the responsibility won't be on you?"

When we did that, we would judge whether or not there was really anything to see when looking at the body.

In one case, this lady had been carrying on very badly for an hour or so. She just had to see the body, and she was very distraught. We determined that the body didn't look that bad, so we opened the casket and allowed her to look. As soon as she looked, she quieted down. That's what she had to do though. I find that a lot of people feel that way. They just have to see the body.

William Lee Shannon, Shelbyville, October 25, 2007

CEMETERY NOT FOUND

We were out in the northern part of the county and had to go into the next county. We had the body at the house and knew where that was. However, we had to go to a certain remote cemetery. We knew where it was but we didn't know how to get there.

After talking to several people who said, "I know how to go there," that was good. We had one of the family members to lead the procession. He led us into the biggest dead end you ever saw. By dead end, I mean the road stopped here! The cemetery was not there, so they just got mixed up and didn't know where it was.

That wasn't our fault, but I guess we got blamed for it! Thanks to another family member, we finally reached the cemetery

William Lee Shannon, Shelbyville, October 25, 2007

MISSING CHURCH TRUCKS

This is about a bad situation. We had this funeral and the body was taken home. There was going to be a church service, so we went out to the home and loaded the body so as to move it to the church. That worked out all right.

The problem was when we got to the church and got out to get the church trucks [catafalques or biers the caskets sit on]. Trucks are collapsible. They fold up so that you can carry them with you wherever you go, like from the house to the church. Well, when I went to get the church trucks out, they weren't there. The man responsible for moving the flowers and getting the church trucks got the flowers to the church, but he left the trucks back at the house, which was four miles away.

Well, what do you do! I was really up the creek on that one. I went back and talked to the family, told them what had happened. I said that there probably was nothing here we can set the casket on to hold it—nothing handy in the church, no bench or anything else. So I said, "You are going to have to excuse me, for I have to go back to the house because they were left there and we have to have them."

We still use trucks all the time, on which we place the casket and then roll them along until we get to where we want to take the casket.

William Lee Shannon, Shelbyville, October 25, 2007

AMBULANCE CALLS

The two-way radio came along, and that was a big help to the ambulance business. We would use our call numbers, and if we got into trouble we had a way to get back to the office.

One of my faithful friends, Howard Flood, was always willing and able to go. He was an extra driver we could use. I was qualified in those days with the American Red Cross, and of course I had to use a lot of that in ambulance work, too.

The reason we got ambulances to begin with was because a funeral coach, or hearse, was the only thing big enough to hold a stretcher.

Ambulance service was never a big business venture for funeral homes, even when we got to having ten to twelve calls per month. Doctors used to go to the residence, and that was a big favor. Very few times would they order that a person be taken to the hospital. So that's the reason we got into the ambulance business. We really didn't want to be in that business, but the hearse was the only thing you could use for a cot. So we ended up having two ambulance vehicles.

Soon, they had a way to make a limousine with a side entrance so that you could get a cot with a body into it. A lot of ambulance calls were from hospital to home for a mother and new baby. My how that has changed!

William Lee Shannon, Shelbyville, October 25, 2007

OOPS, WRONG GRAVE

I had quite an unusual situation at a funeral I conducted. We had this lady's funeral, and she was going to be buried in a family cemetery. The cemetery was not very big, probably less than one hundred graves in it. After the funeral service, we took her body over to the cemetery. The first name of this deceased lady's name was Ible, a very unusual name for this area. Of course, the family had told us where her grave was at and that she had a monument up. So the gravedigger said he wouldn't have any trouble finding it. He got over there and got the grave dug.

After her funeral service was over, we went to the cemetery and pulled up. The family said, "That's not the right place." Believe it or not, there was another person with the exact same first and last name of this lady. That lady's future grave was one row up from the one we were to use, and she happened to be at the cemetery!

They were related by marriage, I think. She got a big kick out of it and said, "I know now what my grave will look like when I do pass away!"

Bryson Price, Lewisburg, November 16, 2007

TEETH MIX-UP

We had a death call in the middle of the night a few years ago. We got over to the house and were going to pick this man up and bring him back to the funeral home. The man's wife and all their children were there at the house, so we asked his wife about his false teeth. So she went to the bathroom, and a few minutes later she came out with a little plastic container with the teeth and all.

We came on back and started the embalming process just as soon as we got back. The next morning she and the kids were going to come in to make the arrangements. As they came in, I noticed she had another little plastic jar in her hand. She said, "Before we get started, I need to give these to you. The teeth I gave you last night were mine instead of my husband's. Is there any way at all that I can get those teeth back?" [Laughter]

Sad to say, at that point it was too late. So I guess she wound up having to go purchase another set of dentures for herself, or she may have worn his! [Laughter]

Bryson Price, Lewisburg, November 16, 2007

BURIED WITH PIE

A lot of churches across Kentucky, especially rural churches in this area, still have fellowship meals for the family of the deceased, either before or after the service.

On this particular service, we were going to a little country church. They were going to have a fellowship meal while the visitation was going on. Actually, they were going to have a visitation before the funeral started going on at the church.

Some of the family members had gone on and eaten, and we were standing out front. We got ready to start the service, and of course, [then the] ministers had got up and had the service. Tradition around here is that, after the service, people still pass around the casket to view the body the last time. Well, we got to noticing that as people were going around and when they would turn, they had a grin on their face. We started wondering as to what in the world was happening.

When we got ready to get to the immediate family, we walked up to the casket with them. We noticed that somebody had brought a piece of pie and a fork and placed it in this man's hand for him to take with him! [Laughter] I think it was a family member that brought it in because the person loved pie, and they wanted to give him a piece to take with him. Actually, that was a very sweet thing to do because they really loved him.

We've buried several unusual things like that. We've buried cases of beer, whiskey, knives, and just about whatever you can name.

Bryson Price, Lewisburg, November 16, 2007

Long, Long Funeral Procession

This story is about a funeral procession years ago. We were going to go to Terre Haute, Indiana, for the burial. So we had the funeral service here early one morning. It was going to be a half-day trip driving to Terre Haute for the burial, so the family had said they'd likely just fix themselves a sandwich or something to eat on the way. That was fine with me.

We got started to Terre Haute and were going to Central City, where the toll road was located, in order to head north. Well, I was leading the procession with the hearse, so I paid for my toll through there, then told the lady that this was a funeral procession. She said, "Well, each car will have to pay for their own toll."

I said, "All right," then pulled on up and got on the side of the road.

I noticed when one car came through, then the next one, and all of a sudden I hear a siren and see lights going. Everybody in the funeral procession had run on through that tollbooth until the last one, when they finally got stopped. Believe it or not, he ended up having to pay the toll for everybody!

So we didn't get off to a very good start there. Then, we got up to Henderson, Kentucky, and I start going down through town there and I start seeing lights flashing behind me. I noticed it was the family vehicles and wondered what in the world was going on. So, I saw the shopping area and pulled over into it. They had forgotten to bring their lunch, so they decided they were ready to eat. Well, we ended up stopping, as they were ready to eat.

That was a long funeral procession, but we finally got up there! [Laughter]

Bryson Price, Lewisburg, November 16, 2007

Bikers Give Military Salute

It's very impressive when the military has a funeral. They fold the flag and have a twenty-one-gun salute and other things. It seems harder and harder to get this service with so many of our men and women overseas.

We have a lot of bikers in this area, and we've had funeral services, when forty or fifty motorcyclists were in the procession. They are just super-nice people, but things are sometimes done a little bit differently when you've got a biker's funeral

We had a funeral service and got out to the cemetery. Well, the bikers had likely ridden as an escort. They asked me if they could. Well, they rode on both sides of the funeral hearse going out to the graveside. When we got out there to this country cemetery, the minister got up and read a scripture and had prayer. As soon as he got through and said amen, we heard gunshots.

We got to looking around and saw people diving and trying to find cover and everything else, and these four guys that were on their motorcycles had taken their handguns out and gave this man a twenty-one-gun salute.

That scared everybody!

Bryson Price, Lewisburg, November 16, 2007

TOUCHING MILITARY SERVICE

One of the most touching services we've had took place last year. A young man was killed in Iraq, and it was very remarkable how our community, our county, and surrounding counties came together and supported his family during that time. It took about a week after his death before they were actually able to fly him back to Ft. Campbell. The sheriff's department here in Logan County escorted us and the family down there.

When we got to Ft. Campbell, the military was just unbelievable on dealing with the family. They were so compassionate. As we were standing there waiting and looking up in the sky, they were letting us know about how far out the plane was as it was coming in.

To see the look on this family's face when they saw their son coming back home, not the way they wanted him to, but at least he was coming back home. The honor that the military did, even getting the casket out of the plane, was just really touching to the family and to me, just to see how they cared for one another.

We had close to one thousand people at the funeral. Of course, we weren't able to handle this here in the funeral home. It happened to be during the summer months; thus we were able to use our local elementary school. The principal, superintendent, custodians, teachers, and the school board just absolutely did everything they could in order to help. As a matter of fact, the custodians were there the whole time; they set up chairs and stuff and wouldn't charge a dime because he was in the military. The main custodian is also a veteran.

It's a shame that it takes a tragedy like this in the community sometimes to show their support for one another. That service touched me more than any other service we've ever had.

Bryson Price, Lewisburg, November 16, 2007

WIFE THINKS HUSBAND GOT OUT OF HIS CASKET

Back when I first got started in the funeral business, I hadn't been licensed very long. My father had just had surgery, so he wasn't able to work at that time. We had this man that passed away, and they wanted to have visitation at the home. The funeral was to be held at the church.

That was quite a different experience for me. I know that years ago most visitations were at the home, but that is something we don't have very often anymore, if at all. Well, me and my mother, and a man that was working here at the time, took the body down there to the home, but we couldn't get it to go through the door. The door wasn't large enough, so we got to thinking as to what we would do to get the body inside.

A window was the only way to go through, so we opened the window and got the casket and all in there. They were to have visitation for two or three days. So we went down there every day to check on things to make sure everything was all right and to see if the family needed anything.

The second day we went down there, the wife said, "I'm sure glad you all just got here. He has been out in the field working all day long, and I just now got him back in here to go in the casket." Well, she got to telling all the things he had been doing all day long.

Well, there I was just starting out in the funeral business, so I was thinking, "How do you respond to something like this?"

My mother was sitting there, and we just sort of looked at each other. We went on and let the lady keep talking and everything. Well, the next day we went back and they had this old school bus that was parked out beside the house there, just an old junk bus. When we went in, the lady said, "He was out till late last night working on that school bus, and when he came back in, you wouldn't believe how long I scrubbed today on his feet because of how dirty they were."

She must have had Alzheimer's or something, but she was convinced that he'd been getting up out of that casket and working in the fields and working on the school bus. After we finally buried him, I don't know if he ever came back or not!

Bryson Price, Lewisburg, November 16, 2007

OUTWITTING THE PREACHER

One minister used to always love to say at the end of the service, "We are ready to turn the service back over to the funeral director," or Mr. Crow or whoever was handling the service.

Whether we were at the funeral home chapel or if we were at a church, we would make our way down the aisle and get about halfway down to where we would usually turn and stand and have everyone at the service to stand, but at that point the minister would start preaching again.

After a few times, we realized he did that just to get back at us, just to have us stand there in the middle of the church. We would stop. And, of course, everyone else was seated while we were standing there in the middle of the aisle. He'd preach again for just a couple of minutes, then would say to us, "You all come on now," then just sort of snicker at us.

Well, we finally got to where we wouldn't pay any attention to him, and when he'd start preaching again, we just kept on going. We told him if he was going to preach, everybody was going out while he was preaching! [Laughter]

That got to be a lot of fun with him.

Follis Crow, Glasgow, December 11, 2007

SCARED BY A HUG

I was embalming a body one time at a younger age, and I had to go under the arm to raise the vessels there. I had the arm back when I was standing up close to the embalming table, reaching over for something, and the arm of the dead body was laid back. There wasn't any muscles of the body that were twitching or anything, but when I had the arm propped back, it came loose and wrapped around my back. Just for a quick second it startled me, and I hugged the table pretty hard to get out of the way.

That's the only real time I was ever really startled by that kind of thing. I didn't think he was awake, but just for a second it did startle me when his arm was around my back!

Follis Crow, Glasgow, December 11, 2007

TWINS AND TAXI-RUNS

I had delivered twins one time unexpectedly in an ambulance when I was about nineteen. We weren't expecting the delivery; we were expecting to take the lady to the doctor for a checkup. When we got to the house, she was in labor, and before we could get her loaded, she had one baby. We helped deliver it, then got her to the ambulance when she was still in labor. She had another baby just a few minutes later. We were not in an emergency vehicle; we were just in what we called a "taxi-run," which was a hearse that was converted just for convalescent runs.

Back then, we had one particular vehicle that was strictly an ambulance, and it was either white or red. It had more sirens, bells, and whistles on it, and it was equipped with more first aid capabilities. It was designed to be an emergency response ambulance.

Our other two funeral coaches were hearses that were called combinations. In other words, they were combinations of hearses and ambulances. We used them when it wasn't necessarily an emergency run. We'd make a run for someone that needed to go see a doctor but couldn't ride in a car, or we were just taking somebody from one hospital to another. We called these trips taxi-runs [too], but I guess a more appropriate term would be "convalescent."

Follis Crow, Glasgow, December 11, 2007

FEMALE FUNERAL DIRECTOR HAS HELPFUL FRIENDS

When Milton Mayes decided to stop working as a funeral director at our funeral home here in Owensboro, I didn't like that, because that left it for me to do. But I didn't care, as it didn't bother me to do it. I'd go pick up the dead anywhere they died. If they called me, I'd go pick up the body. If I felt like I needed help, I'd pick up a friend that wanted to go along with me.

We'd come back to the funeral home, take the body in, and embalm it. I'm the one that did the embalming and would do it just like I was supposed to, then conduct the funerals. People would say, "She's not doing that. You know, a woman can't do that!"

But the school taught me how to do it, and I knew how. So, I was doing it. I did it. If ever I got a difficult case that I felt I needed help, I had friends I could call at all the funeral homes in Owensboro, and they were good to me. They did that for me back then and will still come help me if I needed them. If I didn't need them, I wouldn't call them.

My father passed away, and I said, "Now that Dad is dead, I don't want to do my dad."

The son of Kim Davis, a white funeral director here in Owensboro, said, "No, we're not going to let you do that." So they came and got my dad and did him up really good.

My friend, a black lady funeral director from Madisonville, came over and did my father's funeral service for me at Sargo. I was so thankful.

Ruby Taylor McFarland, Owensboro, December 17, 2007

DRUNK MAN KILLED BY A TRAIN

We had a man that was killed by a train while sitting on the railroad track. He was drinking some kind of whiskey called Thunderbird, or something like that. He had drunk almost a whole bottle of it, and he had a brand-new bottle that had never been opened that was located right beside him when the train hit him. The train cut his right ear almost off. It was just hanging there on his head, and it cut his head open up here right above the forehead. He was cut up pretty bad. That happened only about a block away from our funeral home. The family called, and I went over there and got him, then took him to the funeral home and put him on a table.

I looked him over and thought, I guess I can get him together. Anyway, I cleaned him up, and Reverend Winstat was carrying on [a] revival for Reverend McFarland. The church let out when I had got this body in there. Reverend Winstat said to my husband, "I used to help with embalming a little. Do you care if I go over and help your wife out?"

He said, "I don't know. If she doesn't care, I don't care."

So Reverend Winstat came in and looked the body over. We had him on the table to decide what we were going to do with him. We looked at his ear and looked at the big gash across his head, then cut his hair off. When we cut it, the ear was gone. Actually, it was there, but it was gone off the head where it was hanging. Reverend Winstat said, "What are we going to do with this?"

I said, "I don't know, but if we can get it cleaned up enough so we can see which way it should go, we can stick it back on there."

He said, "Oh, yeah, oh, yeah, we [can] do that."

We then sewed his fingers back on and got the ear fixed by using a needle and thread so it could be seen on the right side. After we got all that done, we embalmed him, and he was looking good! [Laughter]

We stitched his head and put the hair back on. People could not believe how good he looked. They were real proud about what we had done. We then had his funeral, and people talked about that for a long time.

Ruby Taylor McFarland, Owensboro, December 17, 2007

DEATH OF THREE LITTLE BOYS

There is quite a bit of reward in the funeral profession and a lot of sadness. I did not share a whole lot of sadness, because quite frankly it brings back memories that all of us as funeral directors and embalmers try to keep in the back of our minds. I can think of several different funerals I've had through the years. One I think about every now and then happened back in the 1960s, when we had a flash flood. Three little brothers crawled up under the foundation of an old house to try to get away from the water where the creek was flash flooding, and all three of them drowned.

It was really a sad thing for the community and for the county I worked in. The family didn't have anything at all, I mean just nothing. And the man I worked for was Billy Engle. I feel I was very fortunate to have worked for the original Engle Funeral Home [with] Billy and Bige Hoskins and all those folks that were there—the professionalism they had. They were very professional, and we shared so much there at that funeral home.

These three little boys' mom and dad just didn't have anything at all. Mr. Engle stepped up to home plate like a lot of funeral directors do, and he provided all three services at no charge to the family. We had a church service, and we had two hearses and an ambulance, all of which were the same color. We put a child in each one, and their ages were like eight, six, and four. The family was just so overwhelmed with what Mr. Engle and the funeral home did to help them.

They eventually did pay those funerals off. It took them four or five dollars a month, but the care that was given to that family, and the love and care they gave back, was probably one of the things that really influenced me more than anything as to becoming a funeral director.

Jay Steele, Pineville, March 1, 2008

PREACHING FIRE AND BRIMSTONE

On a cold December morning we were down at Rowdy, up on Trouble-some Creek [Perry County]. The family had visitations there at the church and were having a morning service. The church was packed full, and the service began. The preacher, who was one of them fire-and-brimstone boys, started in. He was going to town about people going to hell, and you could tell the spirit moved on him.

After about three and one-half hours of preaching from one preacher, one of the members of the family stood up and started singing. Before long, another family member stood up and started singing, and before long the widow stood up and started singing. Then all the family members stood up, and then the church congregation was up and singing. Well, that preacher stood in that pulpit, never missed a beat. He was doing fire-and-brimstone preaching all over the place. I mean he was just going to town!

The senior funeral director looked over at me and said, "Let's go."

I said, "What do you mean? The preacher is not done yet."

He looked back at me and said, "The preacher is done; he just don't know it."

I said, "What do you mean?"

He said, "Let's just start passing the people out."

As I said, it was a cold December day, so we started passing the people out, and the family was the last to go by. During this whole time, the preacher never slowed down. He just kept preaching full throttle.

We loaded up the deceased into the hearse. As I went back to shut the church door, the preacher was still in the church by himself, preaching just as hard as if the crowd was still in there.

That was the first I ever had the experience of what is called "singing the preacher down." What that is, sometimes preachers get carried away, and somebody in the family of the deceased will get up and start singing, and before long everybody in the congregation starts singing. They are trying to give him a subtle hint that they're ready to leave—but in this particular case, the preacher didn't take the hint, and when we left there, coming out of this hollow headed back toward Rowdy, he was still in there by himself, as I pulled the door together, preaching fire and brimstone. Singing the preacher down!

Jay Steele, Pineville, January 20, 2008

First Embalming

This is a story about the first embalming I did. I was working at a funeral home up in the mountains, and the manager's name was Bige Hoskins. He came in and said, "Well, I think you are ready to do your first embalming."

I had worked there for a little over a year, so I was really excited about getting to do my very first embalming, everything on my own.

He stepped out of the embalming room, and I went ahead and set the features; shaved the person; cleaned, then disinfected, and everything. Bige came back in and said, "Well, are you ready to start?"

I said, "Yes, sir."

And he said, "Now you know that this family is up north, and they won't be in for two or three days, or it could be as much as four or five days before we have the funeral, so you'll need to sit him up hard."

What that means is, you may need to allow for a little extra time, so you may put a little stronger embalming fluid in to preserve the body. It's not a means of permanent preservation; it's just a means of slowing down nature's natural course.

Anyway, Bige said, "They won't be in. They've got to come from up north, etc." So I said, "I understand that, and I'll take care of it."

Well, he left, and I raised the vessels and started injecting, and man, I was going to town! Cool injection and drainage.

A little while later, Bige come walking in and he just stopped dead in his tracks and said, "How many gallons of fluid did you put in him?"

I said, "Now Bige, you told me that we had to sit him up a little extra hard, because his family is coming down from up north and it is going to be three, four, or five days before they can get everything worked out. So, I'm setting him up hard. I'm on my thirteenth gallon."

Well, he wasn't real happy, because it is a standard rule to use a gallon of fluid for every forty or fifty pounds of body weight. Well, this little ole fellow didn't weigh more than ninety pounds, or a hundred at the most. To set him up, two gallons, or three gallons at the most, would have been sufficient to set him up on what we call "a little on the hard side."

Well, Bige wasn't real happy about that, and I thought I was never going to be able to embalm a body again. But I can say this with a pride, the dead man was set up real hard—downright mummified.

Jay Steele, Pineville, January 20, 2008

In Case of Snake Handling, Abandon Ship

This is another one of my snake-handling stories. This is the same church as in the other story I told. We had the funeral service and a two-night visitation at the church. The folks like to handle serpents, based on their belief in a scripture in the Bible about picking up serpents and drinking poisons.

The day of the funeral rolled around, and it was an early morning funeral. We knew it would last awhile since there were six or seven or eight preachers, and sure enough it did. The funeral service started at eleven o'clock and went on until about two thirty or three, then started breaking up.

In the normal routine of things, we'd go up and pass the pallbearers by the casket, then pass the friends by, and then the family. Well, as the family got up there, the kids and others were kind of emotional and they start shaking the casket. I was afraid that the lid on the casket might fall and hit somebody on the head. So I walked down the church aisle and went around behind and came up on the podium to be at the head of the casket beside the preachers and began holding the lid of the casket.

The senior funeral director, Julius Steele, came down, and he held the foot of the casket. I mean, that's just how bad they were shaking the casket, and we didn't want them to shake it off the church trucks.

Well, as the family was getting all emotional and everything, Brother Farmer Sayler decided that spirit had done moved on him to handle serpents again. Where I was standing and holding the lid of the casket was about four foot away from where the serpents were being kept in the snake boxes. So out of the corner of my eye, I saw the spirit move on Farmer Saylor, and he reached around there and flipped open the snake box. Well, he pulled out the longest snake I'd ever seen in my life! Well, that snake fell into two pieces, and I thought that he'd killed that doggone thing.

Believe it or not, he actually picked up two rattlesnakes and dropped one. Well, I'm trying to concentrate on where Brother Saylor is going with the one in his hand while looking at the one on the floor coming toward me. I decided that if I could get my foot on the head of the one coming toward me, I'd be all right as long as I just stepped down hard on it with my foot.

In the meantime, I was trying to figure out what Brother Saylor was going to do with his serpent. He walked around to the head of the casket and proceeded to handle the serpent and lay it in the casket because the spirit was moving on him. In the meantime, my spirit was trying to watch two snakes at the same time. And about the time that snake was about to get to my foot, I was ready to kind of ease down on top of his head. Then, Brother Demus Couch picked up the serpent and put it in the snake box.

Well, now I just had to concentrate on Brother Saylor and the serpent he had. As the spirit kind of eased off of Brother Saylor somewhat, he put the snake back up, and about that time, an elder of the church, Malcolm Asher, leaned over and said to me, "Brother Steele, what would you have done if I had grabbed your leg?"

I said, "Brother Malcolm, if you had grabbed my leg, I would have fallen over dead with a heart attack."

Well, after the service was all over with, we were back at the funeral home going over everything at the end of the day to see if we had everything covered. The senior funeral director, Julius Steele, started jumping on me as to why I didn't leave the podium.

I said, "Well, you know, I couldn't get out since I was kind of hemmed in by the deacons and the elders when that spirit swept over everybody, and I just couldn't go nowhere."

One of the assistants said, "Well, I still don't know where Julius went."

Julius then said, "Well, I knew what I was doing. The next time you need to leave, get out of the way."

I said, "Well, you know, I kind of felt like the captain of the ship, and I couldn't let that ship go down without the captain on it."

Then Julius said, "The hell with the ship. Abandon the ship and get out of there when it comes time to handle serpents."

Jay Steele, Pineville, January 20, 2008

Two-Way Radios and Brother against Brother

This is a story that happened back when funeral homes had ambulance service. Remember, that was a station wagon with a big red light on top of it and an on-demand oxygen mask. Well, that also happened to be the first ambulance that had a two-way radio in it. That was a big deal for us, too. It was a government program that put radios in emergency vehicles. The government was putting them in to modernize the mountains, I guess you should say.

We got called out on an ambulance call going to Butterfly Number Two. So off we went with the big red light just a-blinking and an on-demand oxygen mask sitting in the back and a bed pan underneath the cot.

I went to Butterfly Number Two, [as] the folks at the home sent me up on a strip-mining job. Well, now I was beginning to get worried because things have been known to happen to folks up on these strip-mining jobs, and I couldn't decide whether I was going to get waylaid or what was happening.

I went up on this strip job, and when I got up there, there was a bunch of old boys up there, and you could tell they were drunk out of their gourds. Again, I was getting concerned about what was going on here. Well, I just about decided I was not going to partake upon this ambulance call; I was going to leave.

About that time a preacher come out of the mountains, who I knew was a straight arrow. He said, "Jay, So-and-So has been shot up on the hill here. The family called me, and I just got here. I've been up there, and he's been shot about eight or nine times. He's in pretty bad shape, I think. If you'll get your cot, I'll get these boys and we'll go up there and get him."

We got the cot out of the ambulance, and it was about half a mile, probably close to a mile, up on the side of the hill there where this old boy was at. Sure enough, he was laying on the ground, shot all to pieces. But he was alive!

Back then, there was no such thing as training for emergency services on an ambulance. It was always a red light and an oxygen tank, and whoever had a driver's license was emergency personnel. So I was sitting there trying to calculate how I'm going to handle this. About that time, this old boy came up behind me, and his exact words were, "I sure shot the hell out of that old SOB." He had a .45 automatic, and he was reloading the clip.

The mountains back then were filled with good people, kind of headstrong. There was nothing wrong with that. I kept waiting for this old boy to tell me I ain't taking him off that mountain. He kept reloading that clip, and I'm thinking what am I going to do. About that time, thank God for this preacher. He stepped forward and told this old boy, "You need to sit down there and rest a little bit, and let us take your brother off the hill."

Well, come to find out, it was a brother that shot a brother; they were blood brothers, the-same-mommy-and-daddy brothers. He said, "Come on, help me get him on the cot."

Like I said, we didn't have a lot of emergency training back then. It was just get them on a cot and get them to a hospital. So we eased him up on the cot and started carrying him off the hill. As we were walking off the hill, that old boy was still reloading that gun. I'm wondering what was going to happen. We got down to the ambulance and loaded up the patient. So the old boy got right in front of the ambulance, slammed that clip into that gun, and put one in the chamber. I thought, "Well this is it. He's not going to let me go nowhere."

About that time, that old preacher stepped forward and said, "Now, Buddy, your brother needs to go to the hospital. Why don't you come over here, and let's have a word of prayer."

As I said earlier, this old boy had been nipping a little moonshine. Thank God the preacher was there, and he got him off to the side, and kind of motioned to me to get out of there. So I took off, red light a-blazing.

Using this two-way radio, I radioed ahead and told the hospital I was bringing in a gunshot wound and that the suspected shooter was still up on Butterfly Two on a strip site, and would they notify the state police and let them know to meet me at the hospital.

I got down to the hospital and we unloaded the brother, who was still alive. The state police were there, and I told them where it was at, but I didn't know what the brother's name was that shot the brother. They took off.

Come to find out, the old boy had been shot nine times, but none of them were life-threatening wounds. The guy that got shot refused to press charges against his brother, so his brother never did go to jail or serve any time for shooting his brother. Well, I learned that a two-way radio was just as important as headlights on a buzz saw, as far as gunshot wounds and brothers are concerned.

Jay Steele, Pineville, March 1, 2008

One Preacher's Short Sermon

I have participated in some very long funeral services, but the one I'll tell about now was not among those. This funeral was held in the black Presbyterian Church. It was to be a good-sized service, because a lot of people that lived in town, both black and white, would be there because these were always very special events, and this was a special, well-known man. The days before the funeral held a lot of preparation, as family and friends gathered.

The day of the funeral, we brought the casket down front past a large expectant crowd, followed by the mourning family of the deceased. Dwight and I retreated to the back door and went into our comfortable stance, loose knees, arms folded across the chest, with one arm held up by the face, expecting to be there for an hour, or maybe more.

The choir and congregation sang two or three songs, and then the preacher got up and slowly walked to the pulpit, where a very large Bible lay on the pulpit. (It was like a Masonic Bible.) The preacher looked around over the congregation, and with one hand behind him he raised his other hand and hit the Bible hard, and it just flew open. Very slowly, he raised a finger and placed it on the Bible page where it was opened and said, "It says here, if a man die, shall he live again?"

He paused, then slammed the Bible closed and looked around at everyone and motioned for us to come to the altar. Then he said, "I believe he will." Well, that was the funeral service. That was it!

That was the shortest funeral we ever had or ever heard of.

James M. Pendley, Morgantown, March 3, 2008

The Way Things Used to Be

When I first started in the funeral business, it was not uncommon to have three or four preachers. That was before churches were air-conditioned and before funeral homes were air-conditioned. It wasn't uncommon for us to pack a lunch if it were an eleven o'clock funeral. We'd just get out there in the shade somewhere with the windows [down], because you knew you were going to have to be there for a long time. And people were very emotional and everything, so a lot of them fainted. We'd start passing the crowd, but it would take longer to pass the crowd than it would for them to preach the funeral, even if you had several preachers.

Jerry B. Patton, Brownsville, March 3, 2008

Oops, Wrong Teeth

We had a time back years ago when we had several bodies that had lost weight enough that their dentures didn't fit well. Our funeral home hit several of them like that, and one day we got a call from out in the county. It was another one of those deals where the family asked, "How soon can you have Mom home?" In this particular case, the question was, "How soon can you have Dad home?"

So we brought this old gentleman back to the funeral home, and the family was going to give us a little time before they would come. So we had an opportunity to do the embalming before they came to make arrangements and everything. Don Sharer, who was a real character that could generate more things to laugh about than any human I ever knew, was helping to prepare the body.

So as we started embalming and doing other things, including putting this guy's teeth in. When we put his teeth in, they fit just like a glove. We started bragging about how good his teeth fit, and then Don Sharer started bragging about how good the man was looking. That was typical of Don, and no harm to the deceased, but he always made things interesting.

The family came in and we made arrangements with them, but the man's wife didn't come. That wasn't uncommon back then, because people had large families—several children and everything. When we got to the house with the body and everything, the wife came out with her hand over her mouth. She said to Don, "Don, did you put his teeth in his mouth?"

"Oh, yes, ma'am, we sure did."

She said, "It wasn't his teeth; it was my teeth." [Heavy laughter]

Jerry B. Patton, Brownsville, March 3, 2008

Uppers and Lowers

This is another denture story. This happened to me and not too long ago. We got a death call from a nursing home, so we went out there to the nursing home and picked the body up. They had the dentures in a cup, as they always do. We put the dentures on the cot with us, came back, and put the dentures in the mouth. We kept noticing that one of them wasn't fitting too well, but that is not too unusual. So we finally got them to looking okay, and everything was all right. We went ahead and did the embalming.

The next morning, the nursing home called and asked, "Did you pick up ——'s dentures?"

I said, "Yeah, we got them."

"Did you use them?"

"Yeah."

"Did they fit okay?"

I said, "Sure, they fit fine. Why do you ask?"

"Well, we think maybe you've gotten the wrong patient's teeth in the mouth."

I said, "Well, it's too late now. We've got them in, and we're sure not going to take them out!"

Then they called back in a little while and said, "We've got a worst dilemma than that."

I said, "What in the world is it?"

They said, "Well, you've got the right uppers, but the lowers belongs to the roommate."

So, one half was right, but the other half wasn't! [Heavy laughter]

Jerry B. Patton, Brownsville, March 3, 2008

Devoted Viewer Didn't Know the Deceased

In the funeral business, sometimes you have to hunt for something to laugh about. We don't laugh at people or about people. We laugh with them about funny things that happen.

In 1948 I began working at Smith's funeral home and staying at night to be with and help Mrs. Edna. She was Dwight Smith's aunt and his partner in the business. That was before the old family home was remodeled to serve as a funeral home, so one walked right into the office off the front porch.

When we had a body ready and dressed, we didn't put them in the casket right then but would lay them on what was called a daybed. Then we rolled the deceased into this small room where the family would go to view the body.

There was a lady that lived a few doors down the street. She went to town every day, and on her way she stopped by to see who had died. On this particular morning, she came right on in and through the office, saying "Good morning" to Dwight, then went right on into the room where the body lay. She stayed in there a few minutes, then came back out and said to Dwight, who was reading the paper, "Oh, Dwight, don't he look good. Oh, he looks so natural!"

She paused for a moment, then asked, "Who is it?" [Laughter]

James M. Pendley, Morgantown, March 3, 2008

Baby's Death on Jesus's Birthday

This is a sad story. It is about a death call we got one Christmas morning from the local hospital. It was about the death of this six-months-old baby, and that the family wanted to come in and make arrangements. All of us have a difficulty with handling children's services. I thought, I'm not going to cry and I'm not going to let it bother me. I'm here to be the funeral director, and all this. I'll never forget this story because it sums up what we do in the funeral business.

I told this family how sorry I was about them losing their baby, and they said, "John, don't be sorry. What better gift could we give Jesus than our son on His birthday?"

I just dropped my head and cried like a baby.

John A. Phelps, Bowling Green, March 3, 2008

The Shot and the Shooter

As serious and as sad as ambulance work can be, sometimes there will be something that can be laughed at later. One time we were called to a home in town, close to the funeral home. There had been a shooting.

We arrived to find that the man of the house came home and opened the door to see another man sitting on the couch talking to his wife. He decided hanky-panky was going on, so he pulled out his pistol and shot the man sitting on the couch and wounded him. Then the man on the couch pulled out his pistol and shot the husband and wounded him.

That's when they called for the ambulance. So Mr. Johnson (who, like me, lived and worked at the funeral home) and I arrived to find two men with gunshot wounds. We put one on the cot and rolled him into the ambulance, then put the other man on the stretcher and rolled him right in beside the first. Thus, we had the shot and the shooter side by side in the ambulance on the way to the hospital.

I was driving, and Mr. Johnson turned to me and said, "You know, this may not work out too well."

I asked him what he meant, and he said, "Oh, you know, the shot and the shooter." One of the men heard us, and he said, "Well, it's over and I've accomplished what I wanted to!" [Laughter]

James M. Pendley, Morgantown, March 3, 2008

KILLING WAS JUSTIFIABLE

We got called to Dodge City in Butler County on the north side of the river, and I'd better not mention any names. There was a shooting there, and when we got there the sheriff was already there. We had to wait for the coroner to get there, but it was quite evident that the man on the ground was dead. There was another gentleman leaning up against the sheriff's car, smoking a cigarette. It just happened that this gentleman lived right across the road from my mom and dad.

I walked over to him and called him by name and said, "What in the world happened?"

He said, "Well, I shot the son of a bitch. He was going to go in the house and get a gun to shoot me, so I decided I'd shoot him before he could shoot me."

My eyes were probably as big as saucers, but he never missed a beat.

When you are in a community like that, everyone knows everyone, and the sheriff knew that this gentleman wasn't going to run. He wasn't even handcuffed.

Back then you knew who was going to run and who wasn't.

John A. Phelps, Bowling Green, March 3, 2008

PRISONER GETS HOME FIRST

I've got an ambulance story. We had a guy in Edmonson County that actually had chemistry imbalance. He was a good fellow. When he took his medicine, he would tickle you to death, as he was a guy with great humor. Well, he quit taking his medicine and kind of went off a little bit. They put him in jail upstairs. They really didn't take him up there because he was a lawbreaker or anything. Actually, it was kind of protective custody. They had him up there until they could figure out what to do with him, to try to help him.

To be honest, both the sheriff and jailor were afraid of him. Well, his family comes over there and said, "We need to take him to the Veterans Hospital in Louisville, and they're afraid to take him. Would you take him up there?"

The jail at that time was right beside the funeral home, so I said, "Let me go over there and talk to him." So, I went up there, and he was upstairs. I hollered out his name, and he walked over there to the bars and I started talking to him. I said, "They want you to go to the Veterans Hospital in Louisville, and your family has come over there to talk to me. If I take you up there myself, will you behave yourself?"

He kind of winked at me and said, "I'll be fine."

I said, "Okay, I'll be over here to get you in a minute." Then I told the jailor, "Bring him downstairs."

Then I just walked him out there and said, "Do you want to lay down, or do you want to sit in the seat with me?"

He said, "I'll just lay down. That way we'll have more room for the family to ride up there with me."

We went on up toward Louisville, and at that time the Lighthouse was still a restaurant. One of [the other restaurants] was pretty easy to access from the roads and everything, but when we got up there, there wasn't no place to go. So he said, "I'm hungry, and I'd like to have something to eat."

I said, "Okay."

He said, "Well, you just passed a good place to eat here."

I said, "Well, we'll drive on up here a little bit." So I drove up there and stopped at a place where it wouldn't do any good to run to. We got out to eat, and went back, and got in the car, and started on up there.

When we got there, they had everything ready, so I took him on upstairs and they locked the doors behind him, so help me. I watched them lock the big doors behind him.

The next morning, in Brownsville, I went over to a restaurant to get some coffee and everything, and he was sitting over there drinking coffee! He said, "Where in the world have you been all day, Jerry?" [Laughter]

He beat me home!

Jerry B. Patton, Brownsville, March 3, 2008

CHANGING TIMES, CHANGING TASTES

As our society has evolved and changed, people's attitudes and expectations are noticeably changing right along with the rest of the USA, and funeral practices are no exception.

When I started working at the funeral home in the 1940s, almost all funerals were held in the churches. But just a few years before, when Dwight Smith was just starting his practice in Morgantown in 1935, he did a lot of embalming and preparation of the body at the home of the deceased. He would take a casket with him.

A little later on, the practice was to remove the deceased from the home to the funeral home, prepare the body for viewing by bathing, dressing, and embalming it, then take the deceased home for layout, visitation, and funeral. That was the way it was done about 85 percent of the time. Wakes were held at the home, food was brought in by community members, and folks would "sit up" with the deceased, taking turns two, three, or four at a time. The family of the deceased would retire to rest after all visitors left, but the wake, which was attended by two to four persons, would continue through the night.

Most of the people we served were country folk from out in the county, farmers mostly, so changes did not happen quickly. But gradually there was change, and by the time I was working at Smith's in the 1940s, most of the funerals were at church, but visitations were still held at home. These days, we have one night visitation and most of the funerals at the funeral home, while about 10 percent are held at church. Now there are videos depicting the life of the deceased and different kinds of music, and cremations are not unusual. This makes one wonder what next.

All of this reminds me of one Catholic funeral to be conducted by an elderly priest who had conducted a lot of funerals in Morgantown for years and years. He had a young priest with him to help him, as he was about to retire

This family of the deceased and friends had been drinking the whole time. They had brought beer into the funeral home, and at one point we had to ask them to leave. Just before we were to start the funeral, I was informed that another song was by Guns and Roses. I didn't quite know how to break the news to the priests. So, I just didn't have the heart to tell the older priest, but I did tell the younger priest, "There's been a change in music, and it's not good and won't be as funny as one might think."

Well, the funeral started, and we had one song and the obituary, and then the song [by] Guns and Roses. I was not even familiar with the group Guns and Roses, but I did know that it was not a funeral song.

We were sitting in the office during the funeral. We looked up and here came the older priest walking pretty fast, getting out of there. He didn't know for sure what was going on, but he did know he didn't want to be a part of whatever it was.

By the time the funeral was over, probably about fifteen or more people that were in the chapel came out and left. They came out just shaking their heads. The younger priest stayed and gave his talk before we left for the cemetery.

That's one of those things you get involved in, or caught in, knowing it will be controversial but unable to control or change the situation because the family has the say as to what takes place. The clergy is in a tough situation also.

James M. Pendley, Morgantown, March 3, 2008

FUNERAL WORKER FALLS INTO GRAVE

We had an employee here in this funeral home, probably the best employee we've ever had. He is Randy Stuart, and he was excellent. When he made arrangements, he dotted every *i* and crossed every *t*. We never had to worry about anything. He and I took a funeral out to Fairview Cemetery. When I got there, no Randy. He took the flowers ahead of me, and there was no Randy there. I kept wondering where he was at.

They didn't have time to tell me what had happened, and I'm sitting there getting the casket on the grave. I happened to look, and there was a pair of eyes in the grave looking at me. Randy had fallen in the grave, and it was all I could do to keep from laughing. I kept looking at his pair of eyes looking back at me.

He wasn't unconscious. We were pulling right up when he fell in, and it wasn't time for him to get out. But he kept his cool! He stayed right in there.

John A. Phelps, Bowling Green, March 3, 2008

LISTEN TO WHAT THE PREACHER SAID

When I came into the funeral business as a teenager in 1948, customs were slowly beginning to change, and a lot of people in rural communities only used the funeral home services in preparing their deceased for burial—i.e., embalming, bathing, dressing, and grooming—but still preferred to take them back home for a couple of nights' visitation, and to have the funeral at home or in the community church.

The Smith Funeral Home chapel (for funerals to be held in) was built in 1941 and was used by some town families for visitation and the funeral. Gradually, a few country folk embraced the visitation at the funeral home, having at least two days and two nights. Some families still held wakes, and/or some family members spent the night with the deceased, as they had always done.

The black folk in the community adapted to the funeral home visitation and funerals quicker than the white folk. They conducted themselves and the funeral with dignity. They would come into the chapel and quietly sit down—no talking or noise, just respectful presence. They would be there for two to three hours and upon leaving would tell us, "We're going home now and will return at eleven o'clock for the funeral at twelve."

We would know how they wanted the cars lined up by then, and we would be out on the street waiting for them to arrive, dressed in their finest, calm, quiet, and reverent. I was impressed and still am.

I remember this one Masonic funeral service at the black Methodist church. Pallbearers were there with their white aprons on, looking good and putting on the dog! During the Masonic service, the minister was really talking seriously with them, and he stopped as he looked out over the pallbearers. He stood a few seconds there, then walked back to the pulpit and addressed them with these words: "There you all set with these white aprons on, the sign of purity, but they ain't a damn one of you worthy."

Then he went right back and finished up his sermon. [Heavy laughter]

James M. Pendley, Morgantown, March 3, 2008

Town Drunk Helped Out

The black families were very respectful in Brownsville. They never messed the facility up. When they left, you might have to pick up a little bit, but that was it. . . . They made sure that they had means to pay for whatever they bought.

I'll have to say we had a guy that worked for Don Sharer. He never did work for me, but he hung around there a lot as a young man working for Don. He probably helped me more in preparations than Don did. And to be honest, I thought as much of him as anybody and still do.

I saw two different people in this guy. When I was a young man, he was a town drunk, but when we needed him he would always be sober and worked for us. He would take care of things, and he was very particular about everything. He kept everything right up to snuff, and if you left him alone he'd take care of the tents and all that, so you never had to worry about them. They'd be nice and clean. He took care of them and didn't tear them up, and he wouldn't let anybody else tear them up.

As we all know, back in those days when the community people dug their own graves, they weren't too anxious to move a tent when they had to dynamite. Sometimes you'd go out there and wouldn't have hardly any part of the tent left. They'd just blow it to kingdom come and laugh at you when they did it. But in Brownsville, whenever they died, they'd wait until Sunday to have the funeral. So you might have to keep a body for eight days, or something like that, before funeral time.

It took them there most of that week to have conversations on the phone, or whatever, to get everything organized. And once they did, you knew exactly what to do.

Back then they came from Indianapolis and a lot of other places, and everybody came for whoever it was. And you'd always have a big wake, generally on Saturday nights.

We had an organ in the chapel room, and a couple of couches and everything. So during the visitation a certain guy got pretty well loaded down from drinking, and he went back there and laid down on the couch where the organ was. After most people left, a few of them gathered around that organ and sang. Of course, they had great voices. They got to singing "Lord, I'm Coming Home."

My old buddy raised up and said, "Lord, I've been led home a many a time." [Laughter]

Jerry B. Patton, Brownsville, March 3, 2008

OLD BUGGER WASN'T DEAD

This is a story that took place during my early, early days. One of the men in our community was brother to a guy that worked for us. My wife's uncle, Cecil Webb, had a Shell station there in Brownsville. Cecil was the town prankster. He was always pulling something on somebody.

Well, this guy, Old Bugger, worked for Cecil, but Cecil could [not] keep him sober. If Cecil needed him to do something, this guy would be pretty well soused.

Back when we were in the ambulance business, you drove them until they fell apart because there wasn't any money in it. It was just mostly advertising, so you couldn't afford to buy what you had to pay for because service would completely wear them out. I've told a lot of people a lot of times that at the end of those ambulances I got more concerned about the ambulance making it to the hospital than I did the patient.

We got ready to junk one. Actually we kind of backed it out and pulled it out of the way because we weren't going to use it anymore.

Uncle Cecil was working that day, and he got to looking for his helper. Old Bugger had backed the ambulance in the corner, and he'd got hot and passed out.

Uncle Cecil called us and said, "Jerry, do you still have that old ambulance you haven't done anything with?"

I said, "Yeah, yeah, yeah."

He said, "Put one of them old cots in it and bring it up here. Is it still running?"

I said, "Yeah, it'll run. We can't get it very far, but we can get it up there."

He said, "Bring it up here, and bring a couple of sheets."

We went up there and we put Old Bugger on the top, since we had the bottom of it made up. We put him up there in the car and pulled the drapes on him and everything. And the last thing we did, we just laid the sheet over his head, like he's dead! We set there and waited a little while. In about an hour, I guess the car got pretty warm, and he got hot and woke up. I heard somebody screaming, and in a minute the drapes started flying. He was squalling and begging, "Let me out of here boys, I'm not dead!"

Jerry B. Patton, Brownsville, March 3, 2008

DRUNKARD'S VISITATION

We had a guy in Edmonson County who had three sons, and these boys were all drunks. But this old gentleman was a really great guy—a very religious guy, attended church. He wasn't typical of what you'd think he would be for his boys to be what they were. We buried his wife a few years before he died. Of course, he kept order at the funeral home while she was there, and everybody behaved themselves and them boys stayed pretty straight, but he realized there wouldn't be anybody there to keep them straight when he died.

So he got them together and made them promise him faithfully that they would not come to the funeral home any other way but totally sober and that they would not allow anyone else to.

The night's visitation was almost over, and all three of the boys were there. They'd cleaned up and shaved, looked good, and all of them were sober and behaving themselves. They were a little bit nervous, but they were behaving themselves real well.

One of them looked out the side door where everyone comes in at, and he said, "Oh Lord, here comes —— [the town drunkard]." I'm telling you, that drunk was cleaning off both sides of the street, walking up to the funeral home drunk. The boy said, "Lord, have mercy, what are we going to do?"

I thought the same thing and thought this isn't going to be pretty.

About the time this drunk got up there, the boy said, "I know what to do, I'll take care of him, so don't you all worry about it."

When he opened the door, the boy said, "Come on in, we're glad to see you. Dad thought the world of you."

He got to bragging on this guy and telling him how much his dad loved him, and as he walked up through there, he took him up there to see his dad and said, "I want you to see Dad. He really looks nice."

When he got him up there close, he said, "Don't Dad look really good?" But he never let him stop. He just kept him walking, took him right back out, opened the door, and shoved him right through the door. The drunk's visitation probably wasn't more than two minutes.

The son turned around and looked at me and said, "You know, there ain't nothing more aggravating or no more hard for me to tolerate when I am sober than a drunk."

Then he turned around again and said to me, "Or a sober man when I'm drunk."

Jerry B. Patton, Brownsville, March 3, 2008

PALLBEARER FALLS INTO GRAVE

We've all had this experience, where you have a pallbearer that knows more than God. You try to explain to them what the procedure is, etc. I had that experience with this one particular service. It had rained for four or five days, and the ground was just rotten. In times like that, you need to keep everybody back from the grave because it's already caved in once. Well, we got it boarded up, and I'm telling the pallbearers, and this one fellow is just off talking. I got his attention, but he kept telling me, "I've been a pallbearer before. I've been a pallbearer before, so I know what I am doing."

We got to the cemetery, and I had told them to stay away from the grave. Well, lo and behold, he didn't hear that part, and when he got up to the grave, he fell in it.

That's funny enough in itself, I guess, but what cracked me up with him was that I was sitting in the family car, and the family started laughing. I didn't know what they were laughing about, but I looked and here he is with a suit on and he came out of the grave just as muddy as he could be. To the widow I said, "Well, do I laugh, or what do I do?"

She said, "John, I've always heard that statement that says, 'One foot in the grave, and one foot on a banana peeling.' I never thought I'd live long enough to see it."

John A. Phelps, Bowling Green, March 3, 2008

PREACHER HAS LAST WORD

Jerry Patton, funeral director in Edmonson County, had a funeral in Butler County, and I was helping him. This was during a very busy funeral period. There were four or five preachers having a part in this funeral. The first preacher talked on and on and on and on, then finally sat down. Then the second and third also spoke for a long time.

By that time, we had already been there for one and one-half hours when the last preacher had the prayer and said amen. Well, we thought that was all.

Jerry and I looked at each other, got up, and started down the aisle. Then the last preacher said, "Oh no, Brother Patton. You ain't heard nothing yet." [Heavy laughter]

Everybody in the church turned around and looked at us as we crept back to our seats for another round of preaching. We were about to end a funeral service before it was over.

John Phelps, Bowling Green, March 3, 2008

LADIES OF THE ALLEYWAY

When I was in Louisville, we had a funeral of a friend of an elderly group of people that lived in garage apartments, or carriage houses, in the alleyway of downtown Louisville. Before I finish the story, let me tell about the wonderful people that lived along [the] alleyway. An alleyway was just a means of getting in behind these big old houses up and down Third and Fourth streets. These people had a very close relationship with each other, and most of them were either single or widowed. Oddly enough, most of them were women. During the eight or ten years I was there, we probably had two or three of the deceased ladies in the funeral home.

This group of ladies were very close to each other. They had a society of helping each other out. Most of them had monetary means that were very limited, but they all had different degrees of education and background, so time made a difference in their lives. I don't know if any of them had a car, as this was back in the 1960s. Most of them either rented a cab or rode in a bus. They had to adapt to a lot of different changes in their lives. I remember talking with them, and it was a very interesting way of life.

One of my favorite memories relative to these ladies is about an elderly lady that came by to visit the deceased, and she would walk outside and ring the doorbell and ask me to come outside to see who she was. Then she would ask me to hold her blind dog's leash until she went in to view the remains of the deceased person. She said her dog was afraid to be by himself, so she was quite caring about her little animal. I took care of her dog until she finished her visitations.

James R. Moraja Sr., Lebanon, March 28, 2008

DOGS AT FUNERALS

This family had a little pet pooch that attended the funeral. Well, it sat, didn't make any barking sounds, didn't do anything until we went to church and had the funeral service. After that, we took the casket to the back of the church and opened it for viewing as they left the church.

The wife of the deceased [held] the little dog. She stood at the head of the casket to greet everybody as they filed by. The little dog watched everybody and just turned his head as they went by. A man made a move to touch the deceased, and the dog bit at him, just because the dead man was his master and the dog didn't want anybody to touch the deceased. Everybody just kind of laughed. It didn't upset anybody, but it scared the man it bit; yet he understood why the dog bit him.

It didn't upset the wife, for she understood why the little dog bit him.

We had another funeral where a blind person had a seeing-eye dog, and they kept the dog right in the funeral home during visitation because the dog had become such a vital part of the family. A seeing-eye dog is a dog that has been trained to assist blind people with their walking in getting from one point to another.

That was odd for us to have a dog at the funeral home back then. These things happened quite some years ago. I only know of one seeing-eye dog in our community now.

James R. Moraja Sr., Lebanon, March 28, 2003

Living Out Father's Dream to Be an Undertaker

My grandfather, Earnest Boyd Woodruff, died in 1970 when I was ten years old. Being at his funeral was my first involvement in a funeral service. Grandfather lived in St. Charles, Kentucky, and that side of my family used Reid Walters Funeral Home in Earlington, Kentucky. When I saw the funeral director driving his big hearse, I thought he was cool. Later on I thought to myself, what a reason to enter the funeral business!

My father, Earnest Ray Woodruff, died two years later at age thirty-nine. Since we lived in Madisonville at that time, we used Barnett and Strother Funeral Home. One of the young, new embalmers there was Steve Carson, who lived around the corner from our house. Later on I found out that Dad had taught Steve and other neighborhood boys how to throw a Frisbee.

Since my dad died in Hobart, Indiana, while on vacation with other family members, Steve was the funeral director that drove up to get my dad. That was on Steve's honeymoon, since he'd just got married.

A seed was planted in me through my grandfather's and my dad's funeral services. I thought the funeral director was cool. Every day after those two funerals, when we drove past a funeral home, I always looked to see if they were busy with a funeral. A hearse out front of the funeral home told me that. By that time in my life, I felt drawn to funeral homes. I was very curious as to what was behind closed doors in a funeral home.

No one believed me when I told them I wanted to be a funeral director. "You are crazy," people said. But I knew that my dream would come true and that I had a destiny. I'm so glad I did not let anyone talk me out of that dream.

Some twelve to fifteen years later, I was talking to my mother, and she gave me Dad's high school yearbook. When Dad graduated from high school in 1955, it was a custom for seniors to make what they called a class will for inclusion in the yearbook. My dad wrote, "I, Ray Woodruff, will a free ticket to attend the U.E.P.A.B.M (Undertakers, Embalmers, Pallbearers Annual Business Meeting) to any of those who dare to be there."

The following quote was beside his picture: "Accomplishment— Being a Composer of Songs. Fault—Going to Funerals. Ambition—To Be an Undertaker."

Wow, when I read that, I was blown away! I was living my father's dream and did not know it until I saw what was in that yearbook!

Gregory Woodruff, Salem, March 17, 2008

Death in a Mudhole

One Sunday afternoon, we received a death call to come pick up an elderly man who died while feeding his cattle. The twenty or so head of cattle were in a fenced area around his small, wood frame house. He also had sheep inside his house, if that tells you anything.

When we got there, mud was at least four to five inches deep. My coworker and I had on rubber shoe covers, white shirts, and ties. It was all we could do [to] walk without leaving our shoes deep in the mud.

Our county coroner at the time drove to this scene in his Ford pickup truck. When he got there, he said, "Okay, boys, this ain't gonna work." We could hardly walk, much less carry the cot. Besides, we were both also thinking about all this mud we would have to clean up when we got back to the funeral home.

The coroner wheeled his truck over to where the body was, and we loaded him in back. After we did that, the coroner yelled, "Stand back, I'm going to give her hell."

We thought he would bury the axles on the truck, but mud went flying ten feet or better in the air, and cattle jumped out of the way.

What better way to spend a Sunday afternoon!

Gregory Woodruff, Salem, March 17, 2008

Rationale for Becoming a Funeral Director

We opened this funeral home, W. T. Shumake and Daughters, in 1981. I did not have my license yet, as I was working at another job in Frankfort, but opening this funeral home was something my mother had taken on.

I was not happy with the job that I had, and I said to myself that I can't take another year of this. I had gotten married, and life seems to change when marriage comes into the picture. I decided [that] rather than work there any longer, I would do something else. At that time, we had not yet built the funeral home.

There was an existing building on this property. It was a tiny house that had three bedrooms, a kitchen, a bathroom, and a tiny basement. My dad asked me, "Do you think that you would want to live on the property while we're starting to build the funeral home?"

I said, "Sure, but while we're building the funeral home, can we build onto the house so we can bring my furniture in and put it in here?"

My husband and I had agreed that we were ready to move from Frankfort to Louisville, and so we did. We moved in that house while the funeral home was being built. We started with one small building; then we expanded and expanded, and then in 1996 we expanded to this facility here.

Meanwhile, I was working in corporate America and enjoyed my job. I got paid on the first and fifteenth of every month. It was a given, and it took a whole lot to be fired, so we knew we were going to get our money, and I was trying to help out in the evening wherever I could. Then I decided to go to mortuary school. However, my purpose in going to mortuary school was because my dad said to me, "You know, just because you have a job today, it is not guaranteed that you will have a job tomorrow. You don't need to put all your eggs in one basket. If you go to mortuary school, then you will always have something to fall back on."

Well, the funeral business wasn't what I wanted to do, and I thought to myself that I could go to mortuary school with the intent that I will be able to learn everything that the employee that I hire would be able to do. And I said to myself that I will never be held hostage in a situation in which they know more than I do.

On the very first day of school, some of the students had not actually gone into a prep room; thus, I had not actually seen dead bodies that had not been dressed or anything. That very first day of class, they told us that when we went to our practicum where we actually would go in and observe a body being embalmed, that there would be some of us that would actually fall out onto that concrete floor or just pass out from the sure fact that it was a dead body.

There were six of us in our class that went in this group, three guys and three females. Two of the guys are the ones that hit the floor! So, the ladies thought that we were vindicated, that this wasn't really a big deal. Well, from that moment on, I had little or no fear! But I still had not actually planned to be in the business. I had planned to hire the best of the best to run it if I needed to. But I found out in the process of my schooling that the funeral profession was actually my love. I enjoyed it, so there came a pivotal point in my life when I had to make a decision. I still continued on with my regular job and worked in the funeral home in the evenings. I met with families in the evenings and did pre-needs, but felt that I was slightly exhausted and was using the best of me in the daytime; thus I was only giving the families what was left over.

I felt that was unfair, and with age sometimes comes wisdom, and the wisdom was that I felt better about helping families in their crises than I did on the job that was paying me a wonderful salary. But the truth is, we were having a downsizing at our company. And I was all excited because I was sure I was going to be one of those to be downsized, and I was happy because I thought that I would be able to leave and that I will have this extra daytime because I'm part of the downsizing. They called me in their office and offered me a promotion! I thought, well, this is not what I had in mind.

In 1995 my mom had a stroke, and that was really the spiritual part to which I felt obligated to come help out at the funeral home in a more visible sense. After Mom had the stroke, she got better, and that was wonderful. But in 1997, I left the company where I was employed, and came to work at the funeral home full-time. I haven't looked back.

In 1999, I actually took over the day-to-day operations of this funeral home. I'm not saying that it's feast or famine, but I'm pleased. They always told me, "If you would do something for free, then that's the job that you need to do."

So, that's how I got here. By the way, my mother died June 29, 2007, at age seventy-seven. I tell you that because she is dead. She was a woman that never believed in telling her age.

Gayle Graham, Louisville, May 1, 2008

CORRECTING THE RECORD

This story just goes to the character of people. There was a gentleman that had kind of disconnected from his family. He worked at jobs in different places, but he wasn't good at keeping up [and] letting his family know where he was at all times. So, his brother had tried to look for him and found him in this particular city. So, his brother appears on the scene, and he's looking for his brother and asking if anyone knew this man.

They all looked at him and said pretty much, "No, I don't think I know him, but we do have a guy here with that same name."

He said, "Really? Well, that's probably my brother."

They said, "I don't think so."

Well, what came to bear was that this gentleman was very fair in color. His brother was not. So when he came, they did not know that there was a black man amongst them. They thought it was an all-white community. But he had the same name, but they were just saying, "It's probably coincidence."

Well, the brother [who] knew that his brother was very fair in color said, "That's probably my brother."

Sure enough, it was his brother, and his brother died. They called our funeral home and asked us to go make the removal, and we did. Soon we got the death certificate back, and I looked at it and they had listed him as white.

We had to go back and get a correction made to prove to the courts that this was the same man and that it was just that his color was so fair that people didn't know that he was black. So the death certificate corrected his ethnicity.

Granted, when I saw the man, I had my concerns as to whether he was black or that he wasn't. It was just that his brother happened to be a little bit browner.

You talk about mistaken identity! That's the way that story went.

Gayle Graham, Louisville, May 1, 2008

ELDERLY LADY PICKED HER OWN BURIAL CLOTHING

This was probably back in the 1980s, after we had been in business for some time. Back then pre-need was not really big, but people had their ideas of what they wanted and what they needed. In the black community there is something about reverence for the dead.

I had a woman that was up in age who had a daughter that didn't live here, but she had a grandson that lived here. He was a young man. This woman would tell them things, but still they weren't really listening, because she was saying, "When I'm gone, this is what I want," and all that sort of stuff.

She [was] saying, "I'm not rushing to death, but when this happens I want you to be prepared."

So they weren't really responding to her like she wanted, so she called me to be her funeral director and said, "Gayle, I want you to come over here."

I said, "Yes, ma'am." I didn't know what for. When she said, "Come do," we just did it because she had that type of authority in her voice.

When I got there, she was upstairs, and she said, "At the foot of the steps is a box; I want you to open that box, and I want you to see everything that's in that box."

I said, "Yes, ma'am," and got it open. It was a box about the size of a hatbox. Inside of it was a blue polyester dress, and it had some ruffles around the neck of it and they were baby blue color. She said, "Now, that's the dress that I want you to take to the funeral home and put it up so that when I die you'll have my dress. I put my slip, I put my snuggies (she went on to say she didn't wear panties; she wore bloomers), I put my stockings, and do I need shoes?"

I said, "No, ma'am, we don't need any shoes."

Then she said, "Most importantly, look over the dress. I want that corsage to go on my dress."

I said, "Yes, ma'am." Then I looked, and it was plastic flowers. Then again I said, "Yes, ma'am."

When she died, her grandson called me and told me that she was gone. Then he said, "Well, I've got to go find her something to wear."

I said, "Hold on, I've got a box. Didn't she tell you about the box?" When he said no, I said, "Well, you must come to see the box. I've been holding on to this box for five years, so I'm going to open it in front of you. These are the things she said that she wanted to wear."

He said, "Have you looked at them?"

I said, "Yes, I've seen them once, but not to a great degree."

So, I opened up the box, and in there was that blue polyester dress with the ruffles around the neck of it. In the center of the blue dress was a stain that looked like a food stain, where apparently she had eaten and it had dropped to her breast. Polyester absorbs stain, but it doesn't release stain. I pulled the dress out and said, "This is the dress that she wanted to wear."

He looked, then said, "Surely not!" I said, "Well, this is what she said she wanted." Then he said, "Well, at least I know what color she wanted."

So he went out and purchased a blue dress. Then I said to him, "Now, she wanted this corsage on that was made out of plastic, not silk flowers, but plastic flowers." Then he said, "I'm going to get her a corsage that's made of real flowers."

When I said, "That's fine," he said, "How long have you had these things?"

I said, "Five years." And [I knew] because I had written her name on the box the day that I brought it over.

He said, "We had no idea that she had done this."

I said, "She called me one day and told me to come. I went there, and she told me to take this box and put it up some place safe. And I have done just that."

So, at her funeral, she ended up wearing a blue dress, but not the one that she had. And they had got her a fresh corsage because they realized how much she liked flowers. She had tried to tell them about all these things, but they weren't listening, and that caused her to go to another source. That's what she did. She came to me as her source.

Gayle Graham, Louisville, May 1, 2008

PERFECT WOMAN, LEAVES FINAL INSTRUCTIONS

This is a story about a member of our church. I'll have to describe her personality in order to make this story more vivid. She was the woman in our church that really got things done. It wasn't about a lot of discussion, but if it were about something that she saw was needed, she just did it.

We had built our church, and were looking for draperies to go behind the baptism pool or in front of it. The trustees were trying to decide who they were going to send to get the drapes, how they would need to measure them, how long they needed to be, and that was a project that was taking way too long.

This lady was not a forceful lady but was just quiet about doing everything that she wanted to do. The following Sunday, we came to church and there were the drapes pleated the way they were supposed to be. And the trustees were in such a dither as to who did it; they walked around asking everybody who did it. They had not received a bill and never knew. Finally, one of them looked inside the drapery and found the name of the company and called them. That was the way they found out who paid for the drapes.

This lady said that it was taking way too long for them to get some drapes. She said, "You go out and get someone to come in, they do the measuring, they see the color that you need, and they do it." So, that's the kind of person she was. She was inconspicuous and just blended in but constantly supporting things in her own way.

She had had a couple of bouts with cancer throughout her life but always rose to the occasion [when] she was better. And when she was in her good days, she had sat down and wrote a letter to her three daughters and a letter to my mother, who was a funeral director, and she wrote a letter to my dad, who was the pastor.

No one knew about these letters until she died. The only thing she had ever told her children was that "all the papers you need are in this one specific box in one specific place, so before you do anything, you open that box."

Little did they know that they had letters that she had personally written to each one of her children telling them how she expected them to act, what she expected them to do. It was not a last will and testament. It was simply a statement that told them what she expected them to do now that she was gone. It said, "I'm expecting you to act in this order."

Along with that, she sent a letter to my mother, who was the funeral director, and said, "I know that your husband is going to take care of the service, but this is the stuff that you need to know. I have worked long and hard in my lifetime and I expect my girls to go out and buy me a brand-new outfit to be buried in: nothing cheap, nothing shabby, something classic."

Bacon's was a department store back at that time, and it had something called [the] Mother of the Bride section. Their mother wanted them to go to that clothing section and pick out something nice for her to wear, including jewelry. So, it was all to be new.

Now, when they brought these items to my mother and they did not meet my mother's expectations, she had the right to tell the girls to go back and pick something else. [The lady's] words were lifting off the page, and they were funny! She had said, "I never wore anything cheap in my life, and I don't intend to leave here in something cheap."

So she did that to my dad, who was the pastor. She was instructing him as to the kind of service she wanted. It was not necessary for them to praise her for things that she did because they could never get her into heaven nor hell. She said to Dad, "Preach the word; that's all you have to do. It is not to be a eulogy; it is to be a sermon, because some of these folks that are going to come to the funeral will never come to church again."

So this wasn't about her; it was just about her spirit to write that, and everything that she did, she left nothing for interpretation. It was clear. I have yet in my lifetime to see another person that clear and specific about their life. But she did that.

Gayle Graham, Louisville, May 1, 2008

GRAVES OCCUPIED BY ANIMALS

Families used to go out and dig the graves themselves out in the country. Well, we had this family that had gone ahead and dug the grave. This took place within the last thirty years.

They called me that morning and said, "You need to come out here, and come out here quick."

I said, "What's wrong? Why do I need to come out?"

Well, when I went out there, they weren't like my gravediggers, so they hadn't covered the grave over. What had happened is that a skunk had fallen into the grave, and they were debating on how to get the skunk out of the grave before it sprayed.

They made a little noose like a lasso to try to get the skunk out. Then this gentleman made a remark that tickled me. He said, "We'll just put a board down in the grave and let the skunk climb the board and come out."

Well, that wasn't going to work either. Finally, they started throwing dirt on the skunk, trying to keep the odor down. I don't know how they got it out, but we went back for the funeral and the skunk was gone.

That was something, but it wasn't more than a week later that in the same cemetery a deer fell into an open grave. They got it out okay, but when they did, it was wild and really kicking. It was dangerous.

Denny Northcutt, Morehead, May 7, 2008

Pap under Glass

We had a gentleman—a little country man—and I had no idea about their finances or anything, but he was just a farmer that never dressed well and never drove a vehicle or anything like that. Well, his father died, so he called the funeral home to tell us to come pick up the body. So we did, and he came by and we made all the funeral arrangements.

We went into the selection room that contained sort of an antique casket I had just purchased. It had a glass on it. It was made by Boyertown. He walked over to it, then said, "Boy, I'd like to have that casket to put Pap in, because I'd like to put Pap under that glass."

I told him the price of it. It was really expensive. But he said, "I know, but I'd like to put Pap under that glass. So let me go home and think about it and I'll come back."

Well, I figured that when he left he went shopping, but he didn't. He came back in about an hour and a half and said, "Let's go back and look at that casket again."

I took him back to the selection room, and he said, "Yeah, Pap's going under the glass." Then he pulled out fifteen thousand dollars in cash and paid for that funeral, but I wouldn't have thought he had fifteen hundred! I just knew he was an honest farmer.

That happened right here in Morehead, where I am right now.

Denny Northcutt, Morehead, May 7, 2008

Body Taken Home to Rest in Bed

I had an employee that worked for me here when I first started practice in this building here in Morehead in 1976. He was a good employee and was very faithful.

We always started to work at 8:00 AM, but he'd always come in by 6:30 or 7:00. Well, we had had visitation one night, and this lady came to me after visitation and said, "You know what I promised my husband?"

I said, "What?"

She said, "I promised him that at the last night of visitation, I would take him home and put him in his bed."

I said, "All right, if that's what you want to do."

After everybody left, we backed the hearse up, got the cot out, came into the funeral home, and I put his body on the cot. Then we took him home and put him on his bed.

The next morning, about six o'clock I thought thunder had hit the funeral home. It was my employee out there knocking and beating on the door. As soon as I opened the door, he screamed, "Somebody stole the body!"

I said, "Tommy, we took the body home."

He said, "Listen, I've known you all my life and I know you don't drink, but you can't be telling me the truth."

I said, "Yeah, we took the body home and put him in his own bed."

Now, that's a different kind of story! [Laughter]

Denny Northcutt, Morehead, May 7, 2008

Religious Differences

When I first started funeral practice, we had the Old Primitive Baptists, Regular Baptists, and others that used to have what they called "Dinner on the Ground." And when you went out to the funeral, you might as well be prepared to be there three or four hours.

I had a funeral out here in the country in 1978 or 1979. We went out to the church to have the funeral, and we unloaded the body. And from the funeral home to the church, naturally we had a procession. Well, after I took the body into the church, I went out to check the lights on the cars to see if anybody had left them on, so it wouldn't run the battery down.

All of a sudden, everybody came out of the church, and the first thing I did was to run and see if the casket had fallen or something else had happened. What had happened is that the family had gotten a singer from another church to come in. Well, these preachers weren't going to preach with that foreigner there in their congregation. So, that was it!

They all started getting in their cars, and we drove about three or four miles to the cemetery. No other preachers came. When we got there, I said, "Is anybody here a lay minister?"

"No."

"Sunday School teacher?"

"No"

So, then I said, "Does anybody want to have prayer?"

They said, "No."

So, we had the little memorial folders. I said, "We'll take these memorial folders that have the Twenty-Third Psalm on them, and we'll all recite the Twenty-Third Psalm."

So, we recited that psalm, and that was it. We buried the body. There was no funeral service at all. That was it! All that happened just because that singer was of a different denomination.

Denny Northcutt, Morehead, May 7, 2008

CURIOUS ELDERLY LADIES

Back when I was seventeen years old—this is a story that comes to mind. We received a call from out in the county and we went out there, and this lady was ninety years old. Her request was that she not be taken to a funeral home to be embalmed. The family said that was her wishes, so Mr. Yokely and I proceeded back to the funeral home and got all the equipment that was necessary for us to embalm the body in the residence. This was about two thirty in the morning.

When we got back into the house, we were in a little room and had a coal oil lamp. The little old ladies, being like they always are, wanted to see what was going on. They kept pushing the door open and looking in on us. So we decided there wasn't anything that we were doing that we cared for them to see, but we decided we just didn't need to be disturbed. So, in order to get the job done, we set out a couple of bottles of fluid that emitted a pretty strong odor. So needless to say, it wasn't but a short time after that the little old ladies decided they needn't come back to see what was going on.

Charles Strode, Tompkinsville, May 29, 2008

BURIED WITH HAT ON HEAD

This is a story I very distinctly remember. It's about an old gentleman who was a close friend of ours. We lived close to him, and he had been so gracious. He cut the timber, then had his own coffin made. He kept saying he'd like to try it on some day. But we never did get him in it until we proceeded after he had passed away.

His special request was that his hat be placed on his head in the coffin before he was buried. Well, we had left his hat at home, but his son wore the same size hat and he knew that his father wanted the hat put on him before he was buried. So the son just looked at me and said, "I'll put my hat on him, or give it to you to put on him; then I'll pick up his hat at home." So I got down in the grave and lifted the man's body up, and we placed the hat on his head.

He had his coffin made [in] the old style: small at the head, large at the shoulders, and tapered to where it had a one-piece lid. It was made out of yellow mulberry, and it had a nice satin finish on it. He was buried in a two-inch, solid walnut wooden box, made specifically for the size for the casket to be placed in.

He had his casket made, but he personally sawed the timber. The tree from which he got the timber actually fell into the Cumberland River, and he snaked it out of the river, brought it out, and had it sawed out.

Charles Strode, Tompkinsville, May 29, 2008

DISINTERMENT AND SEVERED THUMB

Some stories are about disinterment of human remains. Over the years, people were buried in family cemeteries. After the larger cemeteries became more available, we had occasions to remove remains. On one particular occasion that I remember as quite unique, I was appalled by what I saw and what I found. I was instructed that when I made the removal of the remains to look for a small glass. The man had lost a finger, and it had been placed in a little small glass bottle that had always been kept on the mantle in the home. However, when the body left the home going to the family cemetery, the mother took the glass bottle and had me put it in the casket.

I was instructed that when I removed the casket from the grave after forty-nine years, to look for the glass bottle. I did find the glass bottle, and it had the appearance of a brown root, which was still the bone in the bottle, and there was still a cork in the bottle. It had been placed on the shelf in a bottle of alcohol, but there was no fluid in the bottle. However, it did look like a brown root but it was a thumb joint that had been severed.

We found that when we disinterred the body and reinterred it. It was quite interesting to look at.

Charles Strode, Tompkinsville, May 29, 2008

VETERAN BURIED WITH STOLEN ENEMY WRISTWATCH

This is a situation in which a gentleman had been buried in another county and his family wanted to bring him back to Monroe County. When we were making the removal, I had a couple of gentlemen who were helping me disinter the body, and at that time it was all done by hand with a pick and shovel. That's the only way we could get into the grave.

When I got down to the grave site, one gentleman said, "I don't know why they buried a flag in this grave."

I said, "Get out and let me look and see." Well, what I found was a red, white, and blue yarn sock that had been placed on the gentleman, and what was on the inside of it was the main femur bone of the right leg that was still in the sock, and the foot bones were still inside the wool sock.

Then I proceeded farther up and found a watch. It looked like stainless steel and had very little deterioration on it. When I picked the watch up, I looked at the time, and the time on the watch was twenty minutes till ten. Then I looked at my watch, and believe it or not, it was twenty minutes till ten!

As I headed back for the burial, a gentleman came by and said, "This man and I served in World War II together." Then he showed me a stainless steel wristwatch that he had on his arm and was still running. He said, "We made a raid after a skirmish in a battle overseas, and there were German generals. We confiscated watches, coins, and knives. I know we both got the same watch."

I said, "Would you like to see the watch he had?"

So I did show the gentleman the watch, and he identified it as being the same watch they took off of a German general during World War II.

It was so ironic that when I picked up the watch, it was still twenty minutes till ten, and it was still legible on the hands of everything. That just blew my mind!

Charles Strode, Tompkinsville, May 29, 2008

AMEN FOR FUNERAL DIRECTOR

One funeral that I very distinctly remember was that of a middle-age minister who was very well liked. He was from [an] African American sect, and we had a lot of visiting brothers that wanted to come to his service. They informed me that there would be nine ministers that would be participating. And there would also be an additional choir group that would come to provide the music and the singing.

Their church had a very small organ, and their piano wasn't very suitable, so they borrowed an organ from my funeral home. [A] lady played it, and I'd never heard the organ sound that good before or after. She started playing continuously when we proceeded into the funeral home, from the funeral home to the church. When we moved into the church, these nine speakers was always up speaking. Each one would speak from three to five minutes. Then when I got ready to pass the crowd, if someone decided they didn't want to go around, or if they did go around and had a little trouble, there was always an usher there to grab them and escort them out of the building.

The preacher came to me and said, "This being the first time that I have worked with you as a young funeral director, I really think that we need to go somewhere and meditate and pray about this."

I said, "Well, we can go upstairs to my office and talk about it."

When we left the funeral home and got to the church, he said, "We have been in the upper room, and we know that our brother is at rest. We prayed about it before we came to the service."

When he made the comment, there were about two hundred people there, and only my wife and one other white person at the funeral. The preacher said, "Everybody that thanks this funeral director is doing a good job, say amen."

Well, I could have gone through a hole if there had been a hole in the floor, as only two or three in the building shouted it out. Then he said, "I don't like that. I want *everybody* to say amen." Well, they did!

It was kind of embarrassing on my part, but he gave me a big plug. So, I appreciated that, as that was quite an experience.

Charles Strode, Tompkinsville, May 29, 2008

A Prayer and a Drink

This is another experience I recall: . . . The preacher couldn't go to the cemetery with us, so we had the benediction in the funeral home, then went to the famous Coe Ridge in Cumberland County. We proceeded as far as we could go, and I knew that there was a fugitive that had broke out of jail and was probably in the vicinity. As I proceeded down the road, I looked up and spotted a state policeman in [unintelligible] gear in a tree with field glasses. I knew he was watching me.

We got as far as we could go with our funeral car, then we unloaded the casket and put it into a four-wheel-drive pickup truck because we had to go up this real steep hill. When we got up there, I thought we had already had the benediction at the funeral home. One of the good brothers said to me, "We're not going to bury [her] like a dog. Somebody is going to offer a prayer, and I believe you are appropriate to do it."

. . . I don't know how far my prayer went, but I did offer a prayer in her behalf. When we finished, they all insisted that they fill up the grave with shovels. Then, when we came back over the hill, still knowing that the state trooper was perched in the tree with his field glasses, they insisted that we needed to celebrate.

They opened up the trunk lid of the truck, and there was a Samsonite case full of good moonshine whiskey. They said we all had to have a drink of whiskey, but I said, "I don't drink."

He said, "I said, we're *all* going to have a drink."

So we all had a drink!

Charles Strode, Tompkinsville, May 29, 2008

WINDOW ENLARGED FOR CASKET

This is something that was very exciting to me. The family had come into the funeral home and made the selection for the merchandise. When we got the body ready, they wanted to take it back to the family residence. So, being a small rural home, we got back to the residence and the door was not near big enough to get the casket through. So they said, "Let's try a window. Let's take a window out."

So we took the window out, but we still couldn't get the casket through it. We'd measured, so we thought we could get it through, but we couldn't. One of the neighboring men suggested that we just cut it out a little bigger. So he went to his truck and got his chainsaw and just cut the whole window out all the way to the floor and wide enough to get the casket in.

That was an experience of having to go back and replace the window later after the burial.

Charles Strode, Tompkinsville, May 29, 2008

SHOE MISHAP

This is an experience that personally involved me and my wife, Dixie. I was at a church funeral, and we were coming back. My wife always assisted on bringing the casket out. She would be on one end, and I would be on the other. I was telling the family to get up and follow me out, and Dixie was on the other end but I didn't see her.

She had on high-heeled shoes that caused her to get a foot hung in a register in the aisle of the church. Before I realized it, I had practically pushed her down on the floor with the casket. So, she was almost run over by a casket with me pushing it over.

That happened here in Monroe County. I was watching the family, and I didn't realize what I'd almost done to her. She was almost run over, and her foot came out of the shoe and she left her shoe in the register. So, we then proceeded on out with the casket!

Charles Strode, Tompkinsville, May 29, 2008

DREAM CAME TRUE

One night I had a dream about an individual, and [then] they came in with his body and he was deceased. . . . I came in, and one of the other guys said that he had a heart attack in his home. He is the one that had picked him up and brought him into the funeral home.

That was similar to a premonition, but I've never had enough experiences like that to believe I was psychic. If that occurred every week or so, I would start scaring myself, but it doesn't happen like that.

William Bledsoe, Irvine, September 26, 2007

SAYING CAN MAKE IT SO

We had a long-time newscaster here in town with WIEL Radio. He did the local news, and everybody knew him. His name was Ron Boone, and he was originally from Corbin, Kentucky. He was down here for several days around the first of the year. He said to me, "Bob Brown, if I have to come down here anymore, I'm just going to move my bed down here."

I've had people say that before. Ron and his wife were having a Super Bowl party a few days later. There was snow on the ground, and

Ron was outside scooping snow and had a heart attack and died there in the driveway.

Since that happened, when people tell me something like that I always say, "Don't say that; it might happen." Then I tell them about Ron Boone.

I'll never forget what he said and did. I don't think he thought he was going to die, but he did.

Bob Brown, Elizabethtown, September 25, 2007

Preacher's Premonition

The same preacher that fell in the grave with me had a premonition he was going to die. He wouldn't let them do heart surgery on him until they brought him a telephone in ICU and let him call me. He then called me and his local doctor here before he'd let them do heart surgery. He never recovered from surgery; he died.

When he called me, he just wanted to do normal talking—nothing outstanding and nothing memorable. He just wanted me to know that he was okay. If it went well, it was okay, and if it didn't go well, he'd see me in heaven.

Terry Dabney, Campbellsville, October 13, 2007

Easing Amputee's Pain

This is a story that you might refer to as an old wife's tale, folklore, or whatever category you would put it in. But I did have the pleasure of [helping] a man that had lost a leg from the knee down to the complete foot. It was amputated, and they asked me to come and get it and bury it. I was going to bury it in the cemetery where he was to be buried, and they didn't think he would live but a short time. So they said, "Just go ahead and wrap it up and put it in a box or something. Bury it where his grave will be dug. And at the time of his demise, just put it in the grave and let it be buried with him."

The gentleman lived about three months. When he came home from the hospital, he was in great pain all during the time he was home. He called me out to his home, and he said, "Which way did you turn my foot and the leg?"

It was the right leg and right foot, so I said, "I laid it on the right side."

He asked, "What did you put around it?"

I said, "I laid it on a roll of cotton."

He said, "There is something pressing my big toe. Would you go take it up and do something about it?"

I did go and take up the leg and foot and did turn it over. And when I did turn it over, at that time his wife told me that he said, "My foot is not hurting anymore."

So I don't know whether if was a figment of his imagination that his foot was being moved or whether I had anything to do with it. I know that sounds crazy, but I did personally do that, and then the man died about three weeks later. So I put the box that his foot was in inside the vault.

Charles Strode, Tompkinsville, May 29, 2008

5

MEMORIES OF FAMILY FUNERAL BUSINESSES

~

The stories in this chapter are about funeral businesses conducted by parents and grandparents, primarily males, across the years. Most of the storytellers grew up listening to and working with their parents and grandparents, and they share fond memories here.

Their tales are often humorous and filled with interesting historical details, some about particular funeral practices and events and some about Kentucky cities and towns. One person tells about his father's role in embalming a parrot; another tells the inspiring story of her mother's decision to go to mortuary school and earn a license for the family business. The stories and the storytellers testify to the important influence past generations had on their families, their communities, and their profession.

DAD AND GRANDDAD

Grandfather Edison Hughes came back from Louisville in 1935. He bought [a] one-half interest in the funeral business here, consisting of a horse-drawn hearse and two caskets, for a total of five hundred dollars. It wasn't long until he owned the funeral business and bought a motorized hearse.

My dad, James Hughes, said he could remember his dad loading up his car with what he needed to embalm and then coming and getting him out of bed and putting him in the car still half asleep. When they got to the home of the deceased, grandfather would get everything ready. Then he would come get Dad out of the car and take him inside to help pump. Dad recalls being half asleep when he had to pump the hand-embalming pump. It was a device that looked much like a bicycle tire pump does today.

Before starting the embalming process, Grandfather used a tool to close the deceased's mouth. The device had two prongs on one end that slid into the nose, and the other end had a flat piece to hold the jaw upward. Then it was screwed up much like a vice to close the mouth. After the embalming was completed, the mouth stayed closed and the device was removed.

Today, most embalmers use a gun that shoots a wire into the upper gum and the lower gum. These wires are twisted together to close the mouth. But my dad is "old school." He still prefers to do it the way he was taught. He sews the mouth shut with needle and thread, then goes under the upper lip into the gum and into the left nostril. Then, it is pushed over into the right nostril and down into the upper gum once more. He then pushes the needle through the lower gum and the thread is tied to the beginning and tightened. This procedure provides a more natural look to the mouth area than the wires that are tightened in a bulky knot.

Dad also remembers coming home from nightly school functions to a corpse in a casket laying in their living room. He can still remember going over and peeping into the casket to see if he knew who it was. After looking, he'd close the casket lid and go upstairs and go to bed.

Connie Hughes Goodman, Fountain Run, September 25, 2007

Man Made His Own Coffin

We buried a man that made his funeral very personal by crafting his own coffin. Burford Ford really got into his work. He literally got into it! He had to get in it to craft it for his special size. It was wider at the shoulders and it was as long as he was.

He said jokingly while being interviewed about his creation, "I'm driving nails in my coffin." He really was, but for people who don't know, "Driving Nails in My Coffin" is an old song.

Mr. Ford painted his coffin with black paint, then came into my grandfather's store and told him about the coffin he was crafting. Grandfather said, "Well, you need some handles."

Mr. Ford asked, "But why do I need handles?"

Grandfather answered, "So we'll have something to carry you by."

Mr. Ford thought for a moment and then said, "Well, I could use tobacco sticks."

But Grandfather wouldn't hear of it. He went to the basement of the store and came back with a box of casket handles and gave them to Mr. Ford free of charge.

Connie Hughes Goodman, Fountain Run, September 11, 2007

HONEYMOON IN A FUNERAL HOME

My father met my mother at a funeral in a cemetery. Later, Dad proposed to Mother in a cemetery. They eloped and started on their honeymoon, but Dad phoned home to tell everyone that he'd gotten married. He was notified that his aunt had died and that he needed to return home. So my parents spent their honeymoon night in a funeral home.

My mother later became a funeral director, and she made this statement: "I had no idea what I was getting into!" But she always says it with a smile.

Connie Hughes Goodman, Fountain Run, September 11, 2007

MISTAKEN IDENTITY

When I played the piano here in our funeral home recently, my parents sat in chairs that flanked each side of the piano. I slid around and nodded to the preacher to direct him to begin the service. He started by saying how Mr. Ichabod Snodgrass would be very missed. The problem was that the man in the casket was not Ichabod Snodgrass; it was his brother Enoch Snodgrass!

I looked at my father to the right, then to my mother on the left. I was thinking as to what we should do, so I asked them about it. Dad grinned and Mother bowed her head, and I looked at the congregation to see people all over the house snickering and whispering.

After the service, Dad walked up to the preacher and nonchalantly notified him of his error. The preacher blushed and said he would apologize to the family at the grave site. Well, he did, but before he was finished he still referred back to the deceased as Ichabod one last time.

Dad said that the same thing happened to him and Grandfather at another funeral many years ago. The man in the casket was a criminal, and his brother was a deacon in the church. The preacher talked about the deceased man as if he were a saint, a faithful churchgoer, and a deacon.

I wonder what the family thought about the remarks, knowing all the while the dead man had been a thief and never had been to church.

Connie Hughes Goodman, Fountain Run, September 11, 2007

EMBALMED PARROT

I cannot omit the pranks my dad use to pull. Just because someone is an embalmer or funeral director doesn't mean they don't have a sense of humor. On the contrary, I have found that most do have a good sense of humor. It may be morbid, but nevertheless it is a sense of humor.

Dad was serving his apprenticeship in Louisville. He lived and worked with his good friend Wallace Hatler, who was also originally from Fountain Run. They were working at a funeral home where the owner had a pet parrot. Its name was Peter, and it lived in the morgue. The caretaker always let it out of the cage when someone was going to be around.

Late one night as Dad and Wallace were trying to embalm a body, Peter was up to his old self. Flying about the room, Peter would occasionally decide to land on Wallace's shoulder or on Dad's. He was becoming a pest instead of a pet! Peter swooped down over the body for the hundredth time, and Wallace swung a towel at Peter and hit him. Peter landed on the dead body with a thud. Wallace looked at Dad with a sheepish look and then said, "I think I've killed the damn gomer." Wallace referred to everything as a gomer.

Well, guess what? Wallace and Dad embalmed the gomer! Afterwards, they sat Peter upon his perch in his cage. The next morning, Mr. George, the caretaker, came to clean up and was talking to Peter. He opened the cage, took Peter out and sat him on his shoulder. Peter fell to the floor. Mr. George cried, "Peter, Peter, why you're dead!" Dad consoled Mr. George and told him Peter had died last night and that he assumed Mr. George would have wanted them to embalm Peter.

For years Dad and Wallace would talk about Peter, the embalmed parrot.

Connie Hughes Goodman, Fountain Run, September 11, 2007

Frozen Leg

I can remember Dad [James Hughes] coming home with a mysterious package. It was long and narrow. He placed it in the freezer. I found out later it was a man's leg. The leg had to be amputated, and the man wanted it to be buried with him at the time of his death. Thus, we froze it.

When I had friends to spend the night with me, it was always a thrill to tell them we had a man's leg in our freezer. I've heard all my life that the person who had lost a limb could still feel the coldness or dampness of the ground if that limb was buried before them. I wondered, could this man feel the coldness of the freezer?

One woman who had her leg amputated and buried said that she could feel the bugs eating at it. Could this be true, or is it purely the imagination?

Connie Hughes Goodman, Fountain Run, September 11, 2007

Police Encounters

Police trouble is infamous but a part of reality. My dad has had a few run-ins with state troopers. While speeding in the state of Illinois, Dad was pulled over by a dignified state trooper who asked him, "What's your hurry?"

Dad said, "If I don't get this guy back to Fountain Run, Kentucky, by 2:00 PM this afternoon, he's going to be late for his own funeral."

The trooper smiled and just told Dad to drive carefully.

Another time, Dad was disturbed while taking a nap. It was in the wee hours of the morning and he'd picked up a body and was headed back home. Feeling very sleepy, he pulled over at a truck stop. He didn't sleep very long until a trooper came pecking on the window.

Dad rolled the window down, and the trooper said, "You can't sleep here."

Dad then responded by asking, "What's the difference in me sleeping here and those truckers?"

The trooper then scratched his head and said, "But you can't sleep out here with a dead body."

Dad said to him, "Just watch me." He then leaned back and closed his eyes.

Connie Hughes Goodman, Fountain Run, September 11, 2007

TWITCHING AND BREATHING

The human body is a curious thing that only God himself can totally understand. When the body dies, the muscles and tissues die. But my grandfather, Edison Hughes, used to tell that the nerves don't die immediately. He said that at one time as he made preparations to embalm, a dead man's arm flung to the side. I thought this curious because Grandfather always embalmed in the main artery in the armpit. It was like the man was letting Grandfather know to go right ahead.

There have also been times that different extremities would twitch. I have witnessed this as well as a body exhaling. You see, there may be air stuck in the chest cavity, and upon moving the body around it will escape, as if the person was exhaling a breath.

Connie Hughes Goodman, Fountain Run, September 11, 2007

CASKET-LOWERING DEVICES

Casket-lowering devices have been used for as long as I can remember. Dad had an antique one that he donated to the funeral directors' museum in Houston, Texas. A man there said there was no such thing as a lowering device like the one Dad had described to him on the phone.

Dad said, "If there's no such thing, then how can I have one?"

The man did some more research and found the name of the company that had made it.

Dad also remembered when lowering devices weren't used at all. He said the casket sat upon two boards, and two ropes ran parallel under it. The casket was simply lowered by two ropes.

Present-day caskets are much heavier than the one described. Thus, lowering caskets now would take a lot of strength.

Connie Hughes Goodman, Fountain Run, September 25, 2007

GRANDDADDY GIVES DOCTOR QUITE A RIDE

This has to do with my grandfather. Back when he opened this funeral home, all funeral homes also had ambulances. I think it was in 1974 that the county took the ambulance services over. My grandfather was going out to a call in a home, and back then doctors made house calls. So the doctor was there at the house, and they got into the ambulance, or, I should say, ambulance-hearse, as it was a combination. It depended on whether you were picking up someone alive or someone that had passed away. They kept a cot in that vehicle. The only thing they had was oxygen, so they couldn't administer anything else like the ambulances can today.

Granddaddy had got out there, and this doctor was going to ride back to the hospital with him. That was when they still had what were called suicide doors on the back. And back where the patient was located in the back of the ambulance, there were two seats for either family members or doctors to sit back there with the patient.

This doctor got in there so he could be with the patient, and the ambulance had just started down the road, and the doctor thought he was going to roll the window down. He had opened the door and ended up falling out of the ambulance!

So, that wasn't a very good experience for him, I guess. [Laughter] It's sort of comical now, but at that time I guess he wasn't happy about it! It didn't hurt him very much, and thankfully, the patient wasn't in an emergency situation.

I guess the funeral homes got into the ambulance service because they were one of the few businesses that small towns had that had a vehicle that could be used to actually transport sick people, since it had a cot that a sick person could actually use.

Bryson Price, Lewisburg, November 16, 2007

YOUNG SON WATCHING FATHER

My dad died when I was twelve years old, but as a young boy age seven, eight, nine, ten, eleven years old, I rode with him quite often in the middle of the night. He would get me up to go with him on a wreck or some emergency run somewhere. It was a lot of fun at that point of time. I think he needed me as his company, and also he was teaching me things about the funeral profession. I'm sure he grew up [working], as a lot of children did back in the 1920s [and] '30s. When they had an opportunity, they would be on the farm working, as farming was their parents' business.

So Dad would take me along to show me what it was like. I don't quite remember this, but I can remember him telling me that when I was two or three years old, he sat me on a stool in the preparation room and

I would watch the embalming he did. Seeing somebody being embalmed didn't bother me, and I never thought anything about it. Of course, I'm sure he didn't take me in when some gruesome accidents had taken place, but I was brought up just around it and never gave it a second thought. I just felt like it was probably something that everybody did.

Follis Crow, Glasgow, December 11, 2007

PREACHER PREVAILS

This story goes back to my grandfather's time. He was very busy at one funeral, and was busy with another one real soon after the first one. Grandfather told the preacher, who was getting ready to start the service, that he was in a little bit of a rush and that any consideration he could give on the time of his message would be appreciated.

The preacher said, "Brother Crow, I love you and think the world of you, and I'll do all I can to help get you out of here on time."

Grandfather used to sit in the back of the chapel and listen to the funeral message. As the preacher was going for quite a while, well, Grandfather got a little uneasy. And [he] finally noticed the preacher had loosened his tie and was taking his coat off and was getting a little bit louder and more involved with his sermon.

Grandfather stood up along the wall and finally got the preacher's attention. The preacher knew Grandfather was getting antsy, so the preacher walked around in front of the podium, put his hand on the podium, then slapped it and said, "Brother Crow, I love you, but I love the Lord better." He preached another thirty minutes.

When I heard that story, I learned at an early age not to try to tell the preacher how to do the service. [Laughter]

Follis Crow, Glasgow, December 11, 2007

WRONG QUESTION

I can remember my grandfather. He smoked a cigar, and I can remember him standing on the porch. I can also remember going with him to cattle sales at the stockyard, because he also farmed.

People used to remember him standing on the street corner on the square. If he weren't busy here at the funeral home, he would always go up there. My uncle used to tell me that Grandfather would say, "Well, nothing is going on, so I'm going up on the square to see if there are any people I don't know."

So he would go up there, then come back, and they would ask him who all he had seen. He would say, "Well, I didn't see anybody I didn't know today."

He would stand on the corner there on the courthouse square and just greet people while standing there. But in those days, people did hang out on the square more than they do now.

One day, my grandfather was standing outside the George J. Drugstore, and Dr. Richards came walking along. He was a local physician that was a cousin to either my grandfather or my grandmother. Dr. Richardson said, "Old Crow, what are you doing? Just standing up here just waiting for somebody to die?"

Grandfather, who was pretty quick with his wit, said, "No, I'm just waiting to cover up your mistakes." [Laughter]

I think Dr. Richards just gave up after that.

I've used that story a time or two when I've had a doctor say something to me when trying to tease me.

Follis Crow, Glasgow, December 11, 2007

Multiple Roles for Funeral Directors and Families

In the old days, when my grandfather, my father, and others started doing funeral services, it was not uncommon for them not only to conduct the funerals or oversee the funerals, but they would also preach the funeral and would lead singing. They might be out in the county far off the beaten path where it was hard to get a minister there [or] when the weather might be too bad for them to show up.

Granddaddy and my father would sometimes preach and sometimes do the singing also. I can remember growing up when they would both sing and preach at funerals out in the county and also in churches. They would lead singing, sing solos, and sometimes do a duet. And even my uncle, who is also a funeral director, would sometimes work with them and sing also.

Of course, embalming was often done in homes back then. I've had people to this day tell me, "I remember when your granddad came out to the house and embalmed my grandmother, or So-and-So in the family. He would say to me, 'Come over here and stand to help me if I need anything.'" They were scared to death but would hold the pail if they were draining the blood during the embalming process or [would] go empty a pan or something.

These family members would help them dress or put the clothes on the corpse, or pick them up and put them in the casket, or help unload the casket. They would just draft someone that looked like they were willing and able. A lot of the work was done in the home in those early days.

I never saw the days of embalming in the home. I think that pretty much stopped in the 1940s. After that, everything was pretty much done here at the funeral home.

Follis Crow, Glasgow, December 11, 2007

STRANGE PLACE TO REPAIR FUNERAL COACH

In the old days, my grandfather and others had a motorized coach, but they still used horse-drawn coaches as well. Sometimes they'd go places back off the roads where they couldn't take their motorized coaches too well.

Down in the Roseville-Etoile area, there was a barn that was there recently but I'm not sure it is still there. My grandfather's funeral coach broke down and broke an axle. There was a garage that I believe was called Payne's Garage. It was a blacksmith garage or something like that.

They actually took the hearse, or coach, and put it up on the main second floor. After they got the wheels fixed, or whatever it was they were fixing, it was too big to go back out the door they brought it in through. It was on what we call now a split level. Well, they rolled the coach in through this door, but to get it out they went on the back side, which was a farther drop down to the ground. So, they built two new doors in the side of the barn, then built a ramp, and rolled the coach back down to the ground after they got it fixed.

I know that barn was still there in the 1980s and still had the doors up on the second floor, but nobody knew why they put doors up on the second floor. But they did it in order to get Granddad's funeral coach out of there.

Follis Crow, Glasgow, December 11, 2007

SCARED SOLDIER

I'm not sure how much truth there is in this, but I've heard it all my life. There may be other funeral homes that have had similar things to happen, but supposedly my father and one other worker had taken a patient from here in Glasgow to a hospital in Nashville. It was late at night, and they were on their way back home on Highway 31. The interstate wasn't completed back then.

Veachel Matthews is who I believe the ambulance attendant was that rode with my father, and they had stopped on their way back. Matthews had laid back on the cot stretcher to take a nap on the way back. My father pulled over at a service station along the way, then went inside to get some cigarettes and a Coke. When he pulled over, there was a soldier on his way back to Fort Knox who was asking for a ride.

My father said, "Sure, I'm going as far as Glasgow. You're welcome to ride with me up that way. Just get in the car and have a seat."

The soldier threw his duffle bag there in the seat beside him. He was sitting there waiting for my dad to come back out, and Veachel woke up. He was in the back. When he woke up, he reached up to slide the partition forward, and he said, "What are we stopped for?"

Well, the soldier just about tore the door off trying to get out. He took off running and left his duffle bag in the hearse. It was a hearse, but it was being used as an ambulance. So the soldier thought that something had gotten him really good out of the back of that ambulance. It really scared him!

I had heard that story all my life and that it happened to my dad and Veachel, but it's been around so much that it just may have circled the globe.

Follis Crow, Glasgow, December 11, 2007

INSPIRATIONAL MOTHER

My parents lived in Louisville all their lives. Back in the 1970s, my parents decided they would go into the funeral industry. My parents were of age and had had their own careers. My dad had worked for the E. I. DuPont Company and was also the pastor of a church.

My mother had been the ultimate housewife and only took a job every now and then, maybe working in the cafeteria when we were going to that school or things like that. At that time, in order to go into the funeral industry, it was required that that would be your full-time job when you were an apprentice. You could not have another job.

My dad said he wasn't going to lie and say he didn't have another job when he did. My mother said, "I'll do it. It all sounds interesting."

With her having the entrepreneurial spirit and sort of the front-runner [as] to doing things, she proceeded to go to school. It was a mortuary school at that time, called the Kentucky School of Mortuary Science. It was located at Second and St. Catherine streets. As a matter of fact, the building is still there. So, she proceeded to go to school. She had been out of school for some time, but she decided to take on this endeavor.

The subjects that we cover in mortuary school are things like chemistry, anatomy, biology—some of the sciences that you could actually go through and graduate from high school without having very much of them. Suddenly she was dabbling into areas that were unfamiliar to her. But she was so dedicated to learning that she hired a tutor to help her. When you walked into my bedroom (I was away in school), there was a skeletal body map taped to the back of the door. It was a map of the skeleton system of the body. It was there so that she could go in and close the door and do the circulatory system, such as the hipbone is connected to the shinbone, or just whatever the story would be. It showed the veins, circulatory system, and just everything about the body, so that she could look and see what muscle [was] this way, etc. So, Mother just worked endlessly on getting this done.

When she graduated from the Kentucky School of Mortuary Science, amazingly enough, I was graduating from the University of Kentucky. I was so excited about her graduation! She was actually getting her certificate, and that meant so much to both of us. You would have thought that it was an Inaugural Ball, because of the amount of energy our family showed for her graduation. We were all so excited about that.

Gayle Graham, Louisville, May 1, 2008

Utilizing Mother's License

After Mother received her license, we had a distant relative that had the Swan Funeral Home at that same time here in Louisville, and her husband had died. They asked my mother if she would allow her license to hang in that facility, and she told them that she would.

The desire was always to build a facility out in the Newburg area. My dad's church is in the Newburg area, but there was not a black funeral facility out here. The goal was always to build a facility here. Of course, it would take a little time to do that.

In the process of that happening, the embalmer that we were going to hire for this facility and hang his license here died. After his death, there was a little quandary about what to do now about hanging her license here. A license could hang in only one establishment. So after much discussion, it was understood that my mother would have to move her license to our facility when it was built.

The owner of the Swan Funeral Home was aging, so she just pretty much decided to close down. And so she did.

Gayle Graham, Louisville, May 1, 2008

6

THE BEREAVED

∼

The stories in this final chapter focus on bereaved family members and friends of the deceased. In the course of providing services, funeral directors are in a position to witness a broad array of human emotions and human behavior, some of which is downright startling. The tales that follow range from the heartbreaking to the hilarious, as funeral directors report their attempts to comfort the afflicted, tolerate grand-standers and busybodies, and prevent family feuds. Most often these skilled and compassionate funeral professionals succeeded in helping their Kentucky neighbors pay tribute to their loved ones and continue their own lives.

PROTECTIVE BROTHER

We had a guy that died, and his brother didn't want him picked up for seventy-two hours. He said that he wanted to be sure he was dead, and he was going to sit there on the porch with a 12-gauge shotgun to be sure that nobody picked him up for seventy-two hours.

So I told the family that was just fine, that I was going home, and for them to call me when he was satisfied his brother was dead. And that's what he did. He called me back in about seventy-two hours, and we picked him up then. But that suited me fine after I heard about the shotgun!

Terry Dabney, Campbellsville, October 13, 2007

ACCIDENTAL MISUNDERSTANDING

We received a call from our dispatch office stating that our next-door neighbor had died. We made the removal to the funeral home and scheduled an arrangement meeting with her family for the following day. During the meeting, her husband stated that he thought he had a life insurance policy on his wife and that he would check on it and get back to me.

Late in the afternoon, he came to my office very upset. I asked him what was wrong and he told me that he had been to his local bank to check on the life insurance policy and was told that it would not pay a death benefit and he could not understand why. I called the bank and was told that the policy was an accidental death policy, and I understood why it would not pay as her death was due to natural causes.

I passed this information on to him and he looked at me, stunned, and said, "Ann, she did not mean to die, so it was an accident!"

Needless to say, we did not collect any money from that policy.

Ann Denton, Hardinsburg, November 9, 2007

REARRANGER GOT WHAT SHE DESERVED

We had a funeral service a few years ago, and I seem to recall that the family lived down around Atlanta, at least the majority of them. And I think that was where the lady was located when she passed away. The family brought her back up here and we went to a little country church for visitation and the funeral, which was all going to take place in one day. They had brought an interior designer who was a real good friend of the daughter up here. So we got down at the church and started setting things up. We thought everything was looking good. The flower shop had brought flowers and all.

This interior designer came before the family, and she got to arranging. She not only didn't like the way we had things set up, she didn't like the way the church was arranged. So she got to designing the whole church, moving things around, etc. So she got everything arranged the way she wanted it, and we went up and told her we'd have to move a few things. The way she had it, the ministers couldn't even get up to the pulpit because she had done covered everything up in the entrance area.

She understood what we told her, and we got everything done like needed. Well, the family came for visitation, etc. We went up to the front of the church, and in a few minutes she came up there and stood there looking out. She said, "Boy, those are some pretty flowers over there."

It was a big field right across from the church. We agreed with her that they were pretty flowers, and we all made some conversation. Before long we had to do something, so we walked away. A little bit later we walked back in front of those doors, and we looked and there was this lady . . . out in the middle of the field picking flowers.

Well, what she didn't know was that it was Queen Anne's lace she was picking. Another name for them is "chigger weeds." She came on back and made a couple of little bouquets, and before you knew it, she was scratching all over. There were red whelps all over her. I know she was miserable for some time. We didn't tell her to go over there, but the way she had been in trying to rearrange everything, we thought that those whelps fitted her about right because of the things she had done in rearranging things!

Bryson Price, Lewisburg, November 16, 2007

FINAL FAINT

We have a lot of people who get so emotional they want to pass out or faint. A lot of times we would close the curtains to the public when the family is viewing the corpse.

This one lady was known for her fainting spells, but she would always look back to make sure someone was behind her before she would fall backwards. Someone would always catch her. This lady got to showing her emotion pretty well, and one of our funeral attendants saw her look over her shoulder. Then she just kind of threw her hands back, leaned back. The attendant stepped to the other side. This lady hit the floor with a loud bang! She didn't stay fainted too long. Actually, she hadn't fainted, but everybody thought she had. When she hit the floor, she got up madder than a hornet because we didn't catch her.

So, that ended that situation.

Follis Crow, Glasgow, December 11, 2007

ANGRY WIFE SHOOTS HUSBAND

We've had several fights here in the funeral home. In one case, a lady and her husband got into a fight in the back of the chapel. They got into an argument, so we got the police over here to break them up. They were being separated, so she was cussing and yelling at him. She yelled at him, "When I get you home, I'll kill you."

After the funeral, things settled down. They got through the funeral, but that night at home in Bowling Green, she did shoot him. It didn't kill him, but she did shoot him because she was still mad.

Follis Crow, Glasgow, December 11, 2007

THE WORST FIGHT EVER

About three years ago, we had a service during which the widow of the young man and the young man's aunt kept having words and were going to fight. So the family finally called the police in, and they came over to me and were talking. I said, "I believe everything is settled down. They don't seem to be having any problems now."

I had just barely got that out of my mouth when we heard a loud crash in the chapel. The police officer and I and two of our other guys went into the chapel. These two ladies had each other by the hair, slinging each other around and fighting.

Trying to get to his walkie-talkie to call for help, and also reaching for his handcuffs, the police officer got tangled up in a row of chairs in the chapel. He took out two rows of chairs himself when he fell down, and the ladies took out another row or two. Each of our two funeral workers grabbed a lady and tried to hold them down.

By this time, we had every police car in town, every sheriff's car, and every constable pulled up out front. You'd have thought that we had a shooter involved in the funeral home. I'll bet there were twenty police officers in here within five minutes, and everybody in town were wanting to know what was going on.

Well, we had a knock-down drag-out fight in there between these two ladies, the wife of the man who had died and his aunt. The police officers took the wife to jail, then later brought her back.

We've had a lot of arguments where we had to have police come in to disperse them, but that was the most serious fight we've ever had. It was a mess!

Follis Crow, Glasgow, December 11, 2007

WIVES AT WAR

Several years ago there was a young man killed in a mining accident out of state. Through the years we've handled many different mine tragedies and related deaths. The gentleman had lived with this lady about twelve years out of state, and she said she was his wife. They decided to bring him back home for burial, and so we contacted a funeral home up there to work through the formalities to get him home.

She came down to make arrangements, and she brought this gentleman's daughter from his first marriage. . . . The daughter said yeah, her dad had lived with this woman for twelve years. So, we were operating on the premises that they were a legally married couple.

We went through the details of the arrangements and set up a time for the funeral, visitation, place of burial, casket, and all information that we needed for papers, etc., and everything was set.

About 2:00 AM the next morning, the fire department called me at home and said, "Jay, there's a girl and a woman sitting on the front porch of the funeral home." The police came by and saw them sitting there and said they were wanting to make funeral arrangements.

This was kind of surprising, but we have had people come to the funeral home before to make funeral arrangements when maybe they didn't have a phone or came straight from the hospital before we had a chance to be notified. So I came down to the funeral home and got here about 2:15 AM. As I pulled around the building, I noticed people sitting on the front porch, and one of them was this young sixteen-year-old daughter of the man we had made arrangements for earlier the day before.

So I let them in, and this lady begins to introduce herself as the wife of the gentleman killed in the mining accident. She is his wife! Then the girl looks over and says, "Yeah, this is my real mother."

I said, "Well, ma'am, his wife made funeral arrangements already."

She said, "That's not his wife. They never were married, and we never were divorced, and we haven't lived together in about sixteen years."

So this sort of complicated things. Well, I brought them on into the building and set down and started making arrangements. Whatever the first wife did, the second wife was dead set against it. Of course, at 2:00 or 3:00 AM in the morning you can't exactly make phone calls to find out who is what, where, and when. So we made the arrangements. They changed everything the first wife wanted to do.

We called later in the morning during business hours and found out that the first wife that came in lived in a state that recognized a common-law wife. The state of Kentucky does not. You can live with a woman for fifty years, but if you are still married to your first wife, you are still married, and your second wife is a live-in companion. So, legally we had to abide by the Kentucky legal wife. Well, that went over like a lead balloon, so they got to feuding with each other and both were going to get court orders, etc.

Well, I borrowed one of Bige Hoskins's tricks. He was a really great funeral director. I got all the family together, both the legal wife and the common-law wife, the daughter, and both sides of the family and his family, and set them all down in the arrangement office and said, "Look, we need to go ahead and get ABC buried. You all can fight out your problems afterwards." They all agreed and finally came to terms on the visitation, the place of burial, and who was going to be buried beside him, etc.

Well, they both decided they were going to try to outflank each other, so visitation was set for 5:00 PM for the family to come in. Well, both the common-law-wife and the legal wife both showed up at four o'clock, almost right at the same time. Well, that didn't go too well. Then, during the visitation, the wife who hadn't lived with him in sixteen years gets right up there by the casket and just begins to mourn all over the place.

The common-law wife wasn't going to be outdone, so she moves flowers from the head of the casket. So she is at the head of the casket stroking his hair, while the real wife is holding his hand.

Tensions began to build up, and sure enough they went off like TNT, and the "wife" wife told the common-law wife to get out of the funeral home. But from a legal standpoint, we can't ask her to leave because it is a public visitation. We can't deny anybody access unless they are doing something wrong.

About that time, the legal wife hauled off and hit the common-law wife right square in the mouth. Then they commenced feuding and fighting each other all over the chapel. Finally, their [respective] families broke them up.

One little thing about this fight was that it kind of got me a chance to get them both together, so I pulled another Bige Hoskins thing and said, "Look, if you all are going to be here together, we are going to have to have some harmony, or we'll have to ask both of you to leave." That sort of ruffled their feathers a little bit, but they both agreed to calm down.

Then we had a couple more little tassles between them during the visitation and what not. The common-law wife decided she wasn't going to pay for the funeral bill, and the legal wife said she wasn't going to pay for the funeral bill. We were kind of caught in the middle. . . . Well, luckily the coal company hops up and says, "We will take care of the funeral expenses, but you have got to keep these ladies at peace with each other."

Well, back when this was going on, it was in the early 1970s. Back then, like today, the illegal use of pharmaceuticals was kind of here, there, and yonder, but the big drug was marijuana. These particular folks were in that age group in which they partook of an occasional draw from a marijuana cigarette, or whatever you want to call them. That kind of helped take the edge off of both participating wives, as well as the other family members and friends.

Well, the day of the funeral rolls around, and in our chapel we have two rows of pews and a center aisle. Traditionally, we've always reserved the right-hand side of the chapel for the family, with the immediate family sitting in the front. Well, technically, his real wife—who was grieving pretty heavy by now but hadn't lived with him in sixteen years, hadn't seen him in fifteen years—and the daughter decided they want to commandeer the whole right side. So they gathered every first, second, and third cousin they could find in her family to cover everything. Well, this kind of knocked his family out too, as well as the common-law wife.

So we quickly reserved the left-hand side for his family. Well, they're sort of on the common-law wife's side, so they all set together. Then we got the service started, and we went through the service. At the end of the service, we came down and had the friends pass by the casket. Then it came time for the family to go by the casket. Well, then they locked up! We had a Mexican standoff: the common-law-wife wasn't going up first; the legal wife wasn't going up first; and I felt so sorry for that poor little sixteen-year-old girl.

Well, they set there for about fifteen minutes, and finally the ministers went over and tried to broker a peace with them. They finally talked his parents into going up. So his parents and the common-law wife went up. Then finally the wife and the daughter were the last to go by.

The wife says, "I want this casket closed before I leave this room."

I said, "All right," so we closed the casket and locked it down. I have what they call a key, or a crank, to lock down a gasket-type casket. So I locked that thing down and stuck the crank in my pocket. Then it was time to go to the cemetery.

Well, all of a sudden, the question [comes up] of whose car is going to be first in line. Technically, it has to be the legal wife, who hadn't lived with him in sixteen years, although she was still grieving pretty heavy, visions of dollar signs dancing through her head. You'd be surprised how, in mourning, money helps people to mourn a whole lot heavier than they normally would have. If there isn't a whole lot of money there, they don't mourn near as tough if there's been a little bit of dissension in their life history. But even though she hadn't lived with him in the last sixteen years, she was mourning pretty heavy. And we think that maybe it might have something to do with that insurance money.

Well, we finally got off to the cemetery. And as I said earlier, this group of folks was pretty well into marijuana. We got to the cemetery, and all the pallbearers were all riding in one car. When they opened up the doors to that car, the marijuana smoke just billowed out all over everything. I mean, if you were within five feet of that car, you'd get a buzz on!

So, the pallbearers come stumbling out, and it takes them a few minutes to get coordinated because they had to carry the casket quite a good little distance. They finally got one or two of them that could lead while the others followed. So we put them on the casket and started. We had to carry the casket probably seven hundred to eight hundred feet, and we were carrying it up a little grade. It was kind of hilarious, because we were supposed to go to the right and the pallbearers [were weaving] left. I guess in their mind they were going to the right. So we kind of fought the weaving pallbearers all the way to the grave and finally got the casket placed on the grave.

Well, the legal widow wanted to make sure something hadn't happened to him during the transportation. So, she wants the casket open to make sure everything is there, and what's not supposed to be there was taken out. One of my partners had a crank, so he unlocked the casket and we opened it up. The legal widow, who was still grieving pain, went up there to check everything out. Well, the common-law widow decided she needed to say one more good-bye. She got up beside the casket, and about the time she started to kiss her husband, the legal wife hauled off and smacked her jaws like there was no tomorrow.

The pallbearers, who were getting a little bit more levelheaded by now, grabbed each of the grieving widows and separated them. The legal widow said, "I want that casket locked up." So we closed the casket, and my assistant locked it with a crank. Then she said, "I want that key that locks that thing, because there ain't nobody getting in there to him."

So he hands me his crank and I just hand it to her, not thinking a whole lot about that. Then they decided they was going to sit there and decide who is leaving the cemetery first.

Well, we sat there, we sat there, and we sat there until the pallbearers were kind of back on the real earth again. They come up to me. These guys were pretty nice people. They just liked illegal pharmaceuticals, I guess. They said, "Jay, what are we going to do with these women?"

I said, "Buddy, I can't tell you. You know what happened through the whole service."

So one of them decided he was going to be the Kissinger of the bunch. There was a Kissinger who worked for Nixon at that time. So Kissinger decides he will go over there to broker a deal with them. So they started walking out of the cemetery, and all of a sudden the common-law wife broke the ranks and came back and said, "I want in that blankety-blank casket if I decide I want to come down here and see him." She continued by saying she wants this and she wants that. But what she really wanted was a key or a crank to get into the casket.

I happened to think about the one I stuck it in my pocket. So I reached into my pocket and said, "Here, this is the one I closed it with at the funeral home." So I gave her the casket crank. His legal wife had got the one we used here at the cemetery.

Well, that appeased her, so she got back in the rank and file and headed out of the cemetery. When they got to their cars, they decided they was going to wait out each other, because they were afraid one of them was going to double back and do something. So, finally the father of the gentleman that was killed in the mining accident went over and said, "Would you just do me a favor and start filling the grave, putting the vault on, and everything?"

So we got our pallbearers and put the vault on, filled the grave up, put the flowers on, and as we were getting ready to leave, the common-law wife decided she wanted some flowers to take back to her out-of-state home. Well, here we went again. The legal wife, who by now was grieving awful bad, even though she hadn't lived with him for sixteen years, she just broke out in tears about how bad the common-law wife was acting, etc., etc.

So, finally Kissinger comes in there, and [he] put one of his buddies in the driver's seat with the common-law wife and he put another one of his buddies on the driver's side of the legal wife and left.

Well, you talk about a bunch of undertakers hightailing it out of the cemetery before they came back, we did! And for about three or four days, the common-law wife would call and the legal wife would call. Then the coal company got caught in the middle of it, because as I said, when there is money involved, people seem to mourn all over the place.

That's the end of this story.

Jay Steele, Pineville, March 1, 2008

POURING BEER ON DADDY'S CASKET

This is a story about a funeral I had a few years ago out in the country for a family that kept secrets from the funeral director. Sometimes, whether we mean to or not, people make judgments on other people. Funeral directors do this also. I did so at this particular time. I knew I was in for a ride as I spoke with the family.

This gentleman had passed away in a city [that] I believe was in Indiana. The family wanted a graveside service, which was not unusual, but parts of the service were pretty unusual.

We had the graveside service, had a song, and all went well, nothing unusual. When the funeral service was over, one of the sons of the deceased said, "Tell the gravediggers to kind of cool it for a bit. We've got some things we want to do." So they went to a car and brought a cooler to the graveside, sat down and put their feet on the casket, popped a top, and sat there and drank several beers. Every time they'd take a drink, they'd pour a little on the casket, "cause Daddy liked it, too."

My first impression was "right on" that time. [Heavy laughter]

James M. Pendley, Morgantown, March 3, 2008

GRANNY HAD NO UNDERCLOTHES

This is another graveside story. It happened a lot of years ago . . . in an out-of-the-way cemetery. This gentleman passed away, and he and his wife were raising their only grandson. I don't really remember now, but think this young boy was eleven or twelve years old. His mom and dad were both dead, and his grandparents were raising him. Of course, you can imagine how devastated this young man was when his grandfather died, since he'd already buried his mom and dad.

I wanted to say that, because what happened is funny, but the circumstances certainly weren't funny.

We went out to this cemetery. As it is well known, when you are in a rural area, there are very few graves set up where everything is level. Most of the time, you're on a little sidling hill or something. On this particular day, the old gravediggers were pretty sharp. They took the dirt up the hill so it would be easier for them to cover the grave up. And when the people set down and leaned back on a chair, they was kind of going back to the hills.

They had two or three old mules tied up to this fence, and this dead guy was a veteran. (After all these years, I can go out to a military service, and if they have a firing squad to fire those guns, it causes me to jump. I look right straight at them but still jump.) They had a flag on this man's casket, and his neighbors were there, and all the people were sitting down. So were the dead man's wife and this young grandson. The minister had the committal, and they then turned it over to the military. So, when they shot that first round of fire, the three mules started braying and pulling on that fence, and when shots were fired, that woman jumped.

Just immediately, again when they shot, this woman jumped again. When she did that, her chair folded up and she just fell straight backwards. As you well know, these older women didn't wear underwear because of the diseases they thought that would prevent. She was lying there, just wallowing, then said, "I'll not be charged today," meaning she didn't leave anything to anybody's imagination.

Just about the time she hit the ground, that kid jumped up and said, "Hell, they shot Granny!" [Heavy laughter]

Jerry B. Patton, Brownsville, March 3, 2008

DRINKING FAMILY

Most of the time, everyone shows up as expected, and the funeral goes as planned and is remembered well. But occasionally a family will be remembered for other things, such as the time we had a funeral for a man who had died in Indianapolis, Indiana.

His family loaded him in the back of their station wagon and brought him to Morgantown. They didn't call us, so the first thing we knew about it was when they pulled into our parking lot. They were all pretty well juiced up, even then. They said they wanted us to "take care of the body, the casket, and everything else."

When visitation began the next day, they were all still well juiced up and got into a fight in the chapel, and we had to get them all outside.

Then later, guns were brought into the mix and we had to call the law. About half the family members were put in jail. The remaining family members were the women, and they attended the funeral service without the men.

This family was remembered for their love, not of the family but of the bottle and can!

James M. Pendley, Morgantown, March 3, 2008

GRANDSON DRANK TOO MUCH

We never had a real problem with drinking here, but we've had our moments. We had this grandson that was a would-be songwriter. He wanted to sing at his grandmother's funeral. It was a song he had written, and we didn't have any say in it, so we said, "That will be fine." The rest of the family was reluctant about it, and we kind of got suspicious at that point.

About an hour before the funeral, he kept going outside to his car. We thought he was just nervous, was just going out there to relax. Well, he was going out there to drink, so by funeral time he was pretty well wasted. The name of his song was "Crumbled-Up Cornbread and Buttermilk Days." He got about halfway through his song and he fell off the organ bench!

The preacher said, "We certainly do want to thank the grandson for that entertainment." [Laughter]

John A. Phelps, Bowling Green, March 3, 2008

NEED FATHER, NOT SON

This story goes back to Dwight Smith and the ambulance service. Dwight told me this story right here in this funeral home. He had picked this young man up who had been shot and was in really bad shape. His mother rode in the ambulance with him, and she was telling Dwight to drive faster. Dwight looked at her and said, "Miss Mary [pseudonym], the only thing left to do is to pray."

She said, "Well, Dwight, that's what I'm going to do. I'm going to pray."

When she began to pray, she said, "Oh, Lord, you need to come yourself. Don't send your Son. This is a man-sized job." [Heavy laughter]

John A. Phelps, Bowling Green, March 3, 2008

GRIEF-STRICKEN WIDOW MAKES MOURNFUL SOUNDS

To tell you the truth, I've never told this story since 1995. Don Sharer died in 1995, and I've never told this story because it's not as funny without him being here. It's not poking fun at anybody at all.

The family members of this family we were going to serve were very, very grief-stricken, and they were doing the best they could. This was over in the area where there was a ferryboat that you used when going to their place. When you went over there for ambulance, funeral, or anything, it was a half-day ordeal just to make it over there because it was all gravel roads.

In this particular case, they waited until the ferry opened and went on to find this guy dead in the bed. And it was cold weather. They came over to get us to come get him. He lived about as far from Brownsville as you could possibly get for us to be able to serve. So when we went on back through there, we went on three or four gravel roads, then finally turned on a dirt road. We went just a little ways, then got back there to his house. When we got there, we heard something that sounded like "Yo-o-o-o, yo-o-o-o."

Don said, "What in the world is that?"

I said, "Well, I'm not sure, but it sounds like to me a foxhound running a fox, but it's of a daytime. I thought it only ran at night."

Well, we got out of the ambulance, and neighbors were standing outside but nobody was saying a word. Finally, Don said to one of them, "Is any of the family here?"

This fellow said, "They'll be here in just a little while. Wait awhile; they'll be here."

Well, a little bit later I head that sound going "Yo-o-o-o, yo-o-o-o."

I couldn't tell where the sound was coming from, but I could tell they'd gone completely out of sight and hearing. In a little while, I could hear it, but very faintly. Then it got stronger, and a little later, here they come.

This poor lady who was the wife of the dead man had on some kind of an old coat and her hair was real long. . . . That was the wildest-looking woman I ever saw in my life. She came running up there close to us, and she saw that hearse that we had there to pick her husband up in, and she just went "Yo-o-o-o, yo-o-o-o." Then she went back around the woods again. She ran totally out of sight again. Then, when she came back, all her people got out there trying to flag her down. Well, they couldn't stop her, and all her children were right behind her, trying to catch her.

Well, here she went again, and Don said to me, "What are we going to do?"

I said, "I don't think we'd make any progress towards catching her."

So, we went inside to get this guy's body. We got inside this little cabin home, and there was no heat in there, nothing. I heard something and looked down, and all the chickens were under the house eating corn and other stuff that had fallen from the kitchen down in there. Those roosters and chickens were having a big time eating down there.

We tried to be as dignified as we could. They had six inches or so of quilts on him, and we finally got them and other things off, then put a sheet on him and everything.

Well, where he was, we couldn't get the cot in there. We were going to have to carry him out there on the breezeway and put him on the cot. We picked him up, and just about the time we got him, . . . I heard something go "Oink, oink, oink," and here it come out from under the bed, a big hog that just took the lead right out through there and like to have knocked us both down. [Laughter]

Once we finally got our composure back, we went up there and finally put the old gentleman on the cot, covered him up and everything, then put him in the car. About that time, I could hear her! She was getting closer again. So when she come back up there and saw that hearse again, here she went again!

I'm telling you, she made another round and the same round again. When she came back and saw the hearse again, there wasn't any stopping her. Finally, Don walked up and said, "You know, probably this car is not helping them do anything with her. I'll tell you what, we're just going to go on back to Brownsville and do everything we can for him. When you all catch her, bring her to Brownsville."

But it was the widow that was making that weird "Yo-o-o-o" sound. She was grief-stricken.

Jerry B. Patton, Brownsville, March 3, 2008

STEPSON'S REVENGE

I started funeral home practice in 1959. At that time, we had ambulance service with the funeral home. We had a death call in the community up above Morehead. The gentleman I worked with at that time was a typical funeral director. He was tall, slim, and the model funeral director. We went up together to this house to pick up the lady who died.

It was out in the country in a rural area, and when we got there we took our cot out of the ambulance and took it into the house to pick up the lady that had passed away. The gentleman who owned the funeral home remarked to the husband, "I sure hate to hear about your wife passing."

The husband said, "Yes, it was bad, but it could have been worse."

The funeral director said, "Worse? How could it have been worse?"

The husband said, "It could have been me!"

Well, her son, which was his stepson, hit him up beside the head with a skillet and split his head wide open. So, we ended up putting him on the stretcher and took him down to the local hospital, or doctor's office at that time, to get his head sewed up. Then we went back and got the body! [Laughter]

Denny Northcutt, Morehead, May 7, 2008

BLINKING EYES

This lady was not real happy that we had to bring her mom in to the funeral home for preparation. After we had finished the embalming, we took her body back to the residence. I left there about ten thirty or eleven o'clock after assuring them that everything was okay, and if they needed me, just call me and I would be happy to come back to the residence to assist them any way I could.

Well, about two in the morning, my phone rang, and they said, "You need to come out to the house. The daughter is sitting there beside of her mom and she is totally convinced that her mother's eyes are opening."

Being the young funeral director that I was, I proceeded out real quick to their house, knowing that it was virtually impossible that her eyes would be opening. When I got out there, I realized that the lady had been sitting there about five or six hours, just staring into her mother's eyes and visualizing that her mother's eyes were coming open. There was no sign that the eyes had opened, and it took me about an hour to convince her that her mom's eyes were not opening. The daughter wasn't looking at her mother, but she had got [it] in her mind, and she had got in such a state of shock and frame of mind that she just couldn't sit still. She just knew that her mama was alive and wanted me to get her out of that casket!

Charles Strode, Tompkinsville, May 29, 2008

INTOXICATED WIDOW

This is about a lady that had come into the funeral home and apparently had gotten into the high spirits, or [was] highly intoxicated. When she came in, she kept telling me that there was an odor on her husband that she could smell. All I could smell was like where the body had been embalmed, so I did not detect any odor. But she kept insisting that I should get something and spray the body, so I went and got the appropriate spray to spray around. Then when I turned around, she was just jumped up in the face, so I sprayed her too!

She never did know it, because she was just too intoxicated to know what I was spraying.

Charles Strode, Tompkinsville, May 29, 2008

GUNS AT FUNERAL

I was talking to Marvin Owens, the funeral director at Brodhead, here in Rockcastle County. He told me about a funeral he had about four or five years ago. The man that was dead was an ex-preacher who was divorced from his wife. However, she took care of him. She wanted her former husband to be laid out at a very small rural church.

Marvin said it was a hot summertime. They took the man's body up to the church and laid him out. He said he noticed that there were several people there with guns on their sides.

This preacher had an illegitimate daughter who showed up. They were all mad but didn't even know that she was there. Marvin told his helpers, "Now, if they start pulling them guns out, you get out of here as quick as you can."

He said, "Sure enough, they started pulling their guns [out] and threatening to kill each other, and the preacher that was going to have the funeral got up and said, 'I want you all to set down and shut up. We're going to have this funeral and that's all I want to hear.'"

So, they finally got it over with. But he said that "Times got tolerable." [Laughter]

Billy Dowell, Mt. Vernon, August 27, 2007

FEUDING BROTHERS

People can be real emotional about loved ones. Sometimes they get a little too emotional. This is a story about Bige Hoskins. He was a fantastic embalmer and just a great, great funeral director. Anyway, Bige was waiting on this family that was feuding a little bit with each other. Actually, they were really coming to blows. They were trying to make arrangements, and one was swinging at another. Finally, Bige stood up and said, "Folks, you know Daddy's dead, and there's nothing we can do about that, and there's nothing we can do about the problems you are having right now. But what we can do is call a truce here. You all set your disagreements aside, so we can get your daddy buried. Now, let's have the funeral and get everything over with, and when it's done you all can just fight it out, whatever you need to do. But let's stop this arguing and fighting and bickering during the service."

Well, they declared a truce, and everything went pretty good with the visitation and with the funeral. They got out to the cemetery. The minister did the committal; then he said, "Shall we pray?"

Everybody bowed their heads and the minister started praying. Just as soon as he said amen, we heard this "wop."

As we looked up from our prayer, one brother grabbed a shovel and hit the other brother right up beside the head with the shovel. Then they commenced fighting each other all over that hillside. Bige looked over at his assistant and said, "Well, at least they waited until everything was all said and done."

About that time, Bige handed the young man [helping him] the shovel and said, "I'm going to help you put him in the ground."

Back then they were using lowering devices, which we don't use a whole lot of anymore. He said, "I'll help you get him in the ground and put the lid on the box," which meant the wooden box.

When Bige left that hillside, the two brothers were still fighting each other all over that hillside, and the young man from the funeral home that filled in the grave was me. When I left there, these brothers were still fighting all over that hillside.

Jay Steele, Pineville, January 20, 2008

Biographies of Storytellers

~

William E. Bledsoe

A native of Estill County, William E. Bledsoe was born October 17, 1947, in Good Samaritan Hospital, Lexington. His mother and her ancestors lived in Estill County across the years. His father was a native of Carter County. Bledsoe began working part-time in the funeral business around 1967, then was licensed as a funeral director in the early 1980s. As part owner of the Lewis Funeral Home, Bledsoe has personally operated this funeral service business since the early 1990s.

Bledsoe's father was not a funeral director, but as a young boy he worked for a funeral director in Olive Hill, Carter County.

Bob Brown

Bob Brown, a native of the Radcliff area born March 9, 1940, owns and operates the Brown Funeral Home in Elizabethtown and has worked there since 1972. He first worked at another funeral home in Elizabethtown prior to attending the Kentucky School of Embalming in Louisville from 1959 to 1960. He became an embalmer in 1962 and served as an apprentice in Brandenburg. He got married while there, then went back to Elizabethtown in 1963 and began working at the Dixon-Atwood-Adkins Funeral Home. In 1966 he temporarily interrupted his funeral service career and worked in the post office and as a mail carrier. He then worked at the Perry and Alvey Funeral Home for five years before founding the Brown Funeral Home in 1972. He has five children, two of whom work at the funeral home as licensed funeral directors.

Brown says this about his career choice: "I decided to become a funeral director in 1949, when I was nine years old. My granddaddy Brown, who lived in Brandenburg, died. When that happened, I had a fascination for the funeral business. I decided to get involved, and I continued to think along those lines. There was never a question about what I was going to do when I got out of high school. Later on, I worked at the same funeral home that buried my [other] grandfather. That was the Sturgeon Funeral Home in Brandenburg, owned by D. J. Sturgeon."

Follis Crow

Follis Crow was born October 23, 1952, in Frankfurt, Germany, where his father was serving in the military. After his father was deactivated, the family returned to the United States, and Crow's father rejoined the family funeral business. Follis Crow has carried on the business since graduating from the Kentucky School of Mortuary Science in 1975.

In Crow's words: "My grandfather actually started in the funeral service with his brother, T. W. Crow Sr., in Scottsville, Kentucky, about 1915. They had a general store, and they did embalming and funeral directing out of the store. They later split up and my grandfather came to Glasgow by way of Ft. Run. He was with a Mr. Jones, funeral director there in Ft. Run, Monroe County, a couple of years, then came to Glasgow in 1928 and founded A. F. Crow Funeral Home.

So, we have been going on as a funeral home here in Glasgow close to eighty years. There is still a Crow Funeral Home in Scottsville called T. W. Crow. I grew up around the family business and always figured I would get my funeral director and embalmer's license just because there was an opportunity here. I never believed I would really be involved all my life."

Terry Dabney

Born July 16, 1952, in Campbellsville, Terry Dabney says his parents would have given him anything they had, but they just didn't have anything to give. At the age of fifteen, Dabney asked local funeral director Bob Parrott for a job, and he has worked at the same funeral home ever since.

Dabney describes his early career as follows: "Back in those days, we had ambulance service and would wash cars in our suit and ties. I wore a tie while driving and when I swept the floor here in the funeral home. And I was here during the duration of whatever was going on in the funeral home. . . . I liked the funeral business, so I went ahead and pursued a career. Back then, you served two years as an apprentice. I went to school for one year at the Kentucky School of Mortuary Science in Louisville. After school, you took a test and were licensed."

Dabney married Judy Newton, R.N., March 9, 1974. Their daughter, Tara Brooks, an honor student at Transylvania University, is currently enrolled at Loyola University in Chicago and has worked the last seven years in domestic violence prevention. Their son, Dr. Traver M. Dabney, is an honors graduate from the University of Kentucky and from Auburn College of Veterinary Medicine. They have two grandchildren, Catherine Isabel Dabney and Olivia Brooke Dabney.

Ann Rhodes Denton

Ann Rhodes Denton is a funeral director at the Trent-Dowell Funeral Home, Hardinsburg, Kentucky, and has worked there since 1988, when she became a funeral director. The Trent-Dowell Funeral Home, which was originally located in a store building in Hardinsburg, was founded by R. T. Dowell, who later sold it to his nephew, Joe Trent, and Trent's wife, Libby, who were Denton's grandparents.

Denton's mother and father, Linda (Trent) Rhodes and Bob Rhodes, now own and operate Trent-Dowell Funeral Home. According to Denton, the funeral home once operated ambulance service for the county and ran the county coroner's office in their building. Serving with Denton and her parents is her brother-in-law, Tim Bandy, who also is a funeral director in this close-knit family enterprise.

"I love what I do and have a very happy, full life," says Denton, who is a lifelong member of St. Romuald Catholic Church, where she is involved in several church activities. She is married to farmer Bob Denton, and they are parents of three daughters, Lindsey (Mrs. Gabe Van Lahr), Traci (Mrs. Jay Wilkinson), and Dee (Mrs. Chad Rainville).

Edward Dermitt

Edward Dermitt, born January 27, 1926, worked in the first funeral home in Leitchfield, which was founded around 1900 by his great-grandmother's nephew, Warren Stone. Dermitt chose to become a Baptist minister and began preaching funerals in Jefferson County and surrounding counties. Finally one of the funeral directors made him an offer: "If you are going to be here all the time, why don't you work for me?"

Dermitt began working for the funeral home and also continued his preaching. He says he has preached around 3,500 funerals, driving as far as Michigan and Iowa and never turning down a request, even though in some cases he received no money. "In the funeral work, however," Dermitt says, "we did have to charge for services rendered."

In 1969, Dermitt had to let an opportunity to buy the funeral home go by, but he later bought his current building in Leitchfield and another building in Caneyville. His sons are also funeral directors.

Billy Dowell

Billy Dowell was born at home April 2, 1937, in Mt. Vernon, where he still lives. Both his parents are from Rockcastle County, and they lived on the creek in Renfro Valley. Dowell's father was a blacksmith and farmer and became a carpenter in his later years.

Dowell says he got into the funeral business accidentally: "Sparks Funeral Home opened their business here during the latter part of 1952. I did some flunky work, such as raking the yard, mowing the grass. Mr. Sparks had a lady's body to put in the casket, but he didn't have any help so he hollered to me. That was the first time I'd ever even touched a human body, but it just kind of blossomed from there. One thing led to another."

Dowell attended college for two years and then went to the Kentucky School of Embalming in Louisville from 1958 to 1959. He was licensed in 1960 as a funeral director and embalmer. After working for the Sparks Funeral Home, Dowell and Roy Martin bought it in 1969 and later changed the name to the Dowell and Martin Funeral Home. They sold the funeral home in 1997, but within three years Martin repurchased it. Dowell is retired.

William Fields

Born at home, April 14, 1944, in Perry County, William Fields graduated from M. C. Napier High School in 1962. He chose to become a funeral director while attending Caney Junior College, which is now Alice Lloyd College. Fields says he was something of "a lost soul" in college, but mortuary school "seemed like an interesting field to get involved with."

Fields attended the Kentucky School of Mortuary Science, received his license in 1964, and began funeral practice at the Maggard Funeral Home, in Hazard. In 1965 he moved to the Harlan Funeral Home, where he remained until May 1967. He then moved to Ashland to work in the Steen Funeral Home, and he has worked there ever since. Fields is married to Pebble (Kiser) Fields, and the couple has three sons. Fields says he intends to continue working, "as most funeral directors don't retire; they typically remain in practice until about the day prior to the day they pass away!"

Connie Hughes Goodman

Connie Hughes Goodman was born January 11, 1969, to James Edison and Linda Hughes. Her grandfather Edison Hughes was in the funeral business for fifty years, beginning in 1936. Her father has also been a funeral director for many years, beginning in 1955. Both of them are also licensed embalmers. Connie's mother, Linda Hughes, became a funeral director in 1978. Connie followed her mother, father, and grandfather's dedication to helping community members in times of sad family losses. She has been a licensed funeral director at the Hughes Funeral Home since 2003.

Gayle Shumake Graham, CFSP

Born July 24, 1955, Gayle Shumake Graham, CFSP, received her early education from the Jefferson County Public Schools and her undergraduate degree from the University of Kentucky, Lexington. She graduated from the Kentucky School of Mortuary Science, Louisville (now Mid-America School of Mortuary Science, Jeffersonville, Indiana). The Kentucky State Board of Embalmers and Funeral Directors granted Graham her apprenticeship license and later her embalmer–funeral director license.

Graham began her career as a businesswoman working at the Brown and Williamson Tobacco Company. An entrepreneur, she has been a motivational speaker for high school students throughout Louisville. She has served as president of the Louisville Chapter of NAWBO (National Association of Women Business Owners). She later joined the family business, known as W. T. Shumake and Daughters Funeral Home, as a second-generation funeral director–embalmer. The business was founded by her father, Rev. William Thomas Shumake, and her late mother, Doris

Jean Harbin Shumake, who was active in the National Funeral Directors and Morticians Association (NFD&MA) and served as secretary of the Kentucky Association of Morticians (KAM) for many years until June 29, 2007.

Graham has been a KAM member, president, and chairman of the board, and she presently serves as financial secretary. She is also the NFD&MA public relations officer.

Graham is active in the Community Missionary Baptist Church, pastored by her father. She is married to Gregory A. Graham, also a licensed funeral director–embalmer, who works in the family business and currently serves as KAM secretary-treasurer.

Rayfield Houghlin

Rayfield Houghlin was born August 27, 1951, in Jefferson County. He grew up in Bloomfield, where his ninety-year-old mother, a licensed funeral director, still lives in the same house where she and her husband set up housekeeping. Rayfield Houghlin's father, Ray, graduated from the Indiana School of Mortuary Science in 1942, served in the navy in World War II, and then went to work for Ed McClaskey in Bloomfield, purchasing the funeral home from him in 1951, the same year Rayfield Houghlin was born.

Houghlin describes his own career decision thus: "I attended college at Western Kentucky and graduated with a degree in education. But teachers were like a dime a dozen back then, and my father had a good funeral business going here at home and needed some help. So, I just felt like, with his guidance and his instruction, I could follow in his footsteps, which I've done. My daddy was here all his life. He had a stroke when he was fifty-seven years old, then died in 1980 from cancer. I have a funeral home in Bardstown [Greenwell-Houghlin-Northside], one in Taylorsville [Greenwell-Jenkins-Houghlin], and this one in Bloomfield. I have two children, ages sixteen and fifteen, but whether or not they'll go into the funeral business, I don't know. They help me here at the funeral home. . . . This is the only job I've ever had, and I just try to do it to the best of my ability. I'm also a coroner in Nelson County. I've been a deputy coroner since 1977, when I got my director and embalming license. I was voted in as coroner this last election."

Ruby Taylor McFarland

Ruby Taylor McFarland was born July 29, 1920, in Sorgho, Daviess County. She worked at the Owensboro-Daviess County Hospital for twenty-five years and then began helping out at the Haynes Funeral Home, passing out fans, programs, etc. "I sort of took a liking to it," McFarland says, noting that her husband was Mr. Haynes's pastor. When Mr. Haynes died, McFarland and her husband rented the building and carried on the business, finally purchasing it from Mrs. Joanne Haynes.

McFarland says that Dr. Reginald Claypool Neblett, the only black doctor in Owensboro for years, encouraged her to get her funeral-director license. She went to the Kentucky School of Mortuary Science in Louisville, became licensed in 1973, and served a three-year apprenticeship. She is a member of several professional organizations and in August 2007 was honored by 100 Black Women of Funeral Service, Inc. Two of her sons, Dwight and Alison, are funeral directors and also work at the McFarland Funeral Home, a state-of-the-art mortuary.

Charles McMurtrey

Charles Huston McMurtrey was born December 11, 1925, son of Herman and Hazel (Grider) McMurtrey. After service in the navy during World War 11, he attended the Kentucky School of Embalming and received his funeral director and embalming licenses. He was an apprentice at the Hatcher Funeral Home in Glasgow before returning to Summer Shade to join his father at the McMurtrey Funeral Home.

McMurtrey's father had a cabinet shop business that also made caskets. The initial funeral business in Summer Shade was owned by White, Bowles, and Grider, but Herman McMurtrey purchased it after receiving his funeral director's license in 1928. Embalming was performed by a Hatcher from Glasgow, and a horse-drawn hearse operated by Fount Clark helped with burial services.

Charles McMurtrey married Agnes Arlene Morgan on January 16, 1952. They have six children, who were raised in a home near the funeral home, including Charles Thomas "Tom," David Karl, Janice Faye (Page), Gary Russell, Laurie Ellen (Butler), and Shana Beth McMurtrey. Charles Thomas "Tom" received his funeral director and embalming licenses in 2002 and is now manager of the McMurtrey Funeral Home.

James A. Moraja Sr.

James A. Moraja Sr. was born September 11, 1941, in Springfield, Washington County, to parents, William Cecil and Harriet Ann Moraja. He grew up on a farm with his two brothers, William Cecil Jr. and Joseph C. Moraja.

After graduating from St. Joe Prep, Bardstown, Moraja enrolled in the Kentucky School of Embalming in 1960 and received his embalmer and funeral director licenses in 1963. He worked at the Lee E. Cralle Funeral Home, Louisville, from 1960 to 1967 and then returned to farming. In 1969, he and business partner Lee Wilcher purchased the Bosley Funeral Home, Lebanon, where Wilcher worked. In 1979, Wilcher became ill and Moraja became the owner of the Bosley Funeral Home. He operates it with his wife, Betty; his son, Richard, and daughter-in-law, Pam Moraja; and long-time employee Tom Colvin.

"The reason I became a funeral director is because I like it," Moraja says. "It's a profession that has its own rewards in different ways. You live the life of a funeral director in a small town. You get to know everyone, and everyone gets to know you. You are a funeral director twenty-four hours a day, just like a local doctor is a doctor. I think most funeral directors in small towns have grown to be a part of the small-town community."

Denny Northcutt

A desire to "serve every family as we would like to be served" motivated John D. "Denny" Northcutt to establish Northcutt and Son Home for Funerals, Inc., a family-owned business, in 1976. Northcutt began his career in 1959 as an apprentice and became a licensed funeral director and embalmer in 1963. A 1962 graduate of Cincinnati College of Embalming, he worked for sixteen years in Morehead as an ambulance driver, funeral director, and embalmer prior to establishing his own firm. Northcutt says he realized his dream of building a funeral home designed specifically as such, including a chapel with pews. The business has provided services for a broad range of people, including a college president, a member of the Delta Force, a pitcher for the New York Yankees, and the first fatality at the Pentagon on 9/11.

At age sixty-eight, Northcutt still reports to work at 8 AM daily and most often locks the door during visitation. He gives lectures to college classes, provides funeral home educational tours, has served as president of the Eastern Kentucky Funeral Directors Association, and is currently serving his second term on the Kentucky State Board of Embalmers and Funeral Directors.

Northcutt and his wife, Helen, have been married for forty-seven years. Their son, John, who is active in the family business, is married and has three daughters.

Jerry Bruce Patton

Jerry Bruce Patton was born June 25, 1943, to Nola and John Patton, residents of the Sweeden community, Edmonson County. He graduated from Edmonson County High School in 1961 and from Mid-America College of Funeral Service in 1962. At age fifteen, Patton began working at the Sharer Funeral Home as a gravedigger. At age twenty-five, he purchased the Sharer Funeral Home, which he has operated for forty years.

Patton married Marilyn Webb in 1963, and they have two daughters and three grandsons. He ran the Edmonson County Ambulance Service during his early career and served as county coroner for one term. He is a member of many local organizations and served as president of the

Edmonson County Chamber of Commerce. During the years 1991 to 2000, Patton served in various official positions, including president of the board of the Funeral Directors Association of Kentucky. He also served as Southern District Director (1996–2006) for the Funeral Directors Burial Association and has served as a member of the Kentucky Funeral Directors Burial Association since 2006.

He was recognized in 2004 by the Edmonson County Chamber of Commerce as Citizen of the Year. Throughout the years, Patton has pastored numerous United Baptist churches and continues to serve as pastor of two churches. He was lead singer for the gospel singing group known as the Commanders Quartet and currently sings bass for the Cornerstones, which includes his daughter Andrea Brantley.

James Martin Pendley

James Martin Pendley, son of World War I veteran Clyde Pendley and Annie Martin Pendley, was born in October 1934 in Morgantown, Butler County. Pendley graduated from Morgantown High School in 1952 and served in the navy from 1952 to 1955 during the Korean conflict. Subsequently, he attended Bowling Green Business University until he married June Lee in August 1956. The newlyweds moved to Louisville, where Pendley attended the University of Louisville and worked at the Jewish Hospital from 1956 to 1958. The Pendleys later had two daughters, Joan and Jill, and now have two grandchildren, Turner and Shelby England.

Pendley returned to Morgantown in 1958 and worked at the Smith Funeral Home for a brief period. He then attended the Kentucky School of Mortuary Science, Louisville, before returning to Morgantown in 1960 to start his professional career at the Dwight Smith Mortuary, where he had worked during his high school years. In 1969, James and June Pendley, along with Don and Dolores Sharer, purchased the mortuary and renamed it the Smith Funeral Home. Pendley and Sharer provided ambulance service until 1975, then sold the funeral home in 1980. After a period of working in other positions, Pendley began working again in 1993 at the same funeral home. He retired in 2000 but continues to work part-time for the new owner, viewing his work not as a job but a calling.

John A. Phelps

John A. Phelps says that as a young child, all he ever wanted to wear were black suits, and his parents thought he would be either a priest or a funeral director. That all came to fruition when he started working part-time at the Ayers and Sharer Funeral Home in Morgantown, Kentucky, in 1967 at the age of seventeen. He served his apprenticeship at that funeral home until 1971 and then attended the Kentucky School of Mortuary Science in Louisville. While attending school, he worked for the McAfee Funeral Home.

After graduation in 1972, Phelps returned to Morgantown and started work as a licensed funeral director and embalmer at the Smith Funeral Home. In 1974, he went to Beaver Dam to work at the William L. Danks Funeral Home, but soon he was offered a job in Bowling Green at the Arch L. Heady-Johnson Funeral Home. He started working there in 1974 and after several years became manager.

In 2002, Phelps became an owner of the Johnson-Vaughn-Phelps Funeral Home. Phelps says that he and Gene Vaughn purchased the business and left Johnson in the name of the funeral home as a tribute to Aubrey and Elaine Johnson, who founded the funeral home in 1953.

Bryson Price

Bryson Price was born October 25, 1962, in Lewisburg and was raised there. His grandfather Ryan Price started the family funeral home in 1948. His father, Buddy Price, worked in the business but is now retired. Bryson Price married Susan Marie Holloway in 1983 and has two children, Trevan and Trent.

Price graduated from Lewisburg High School in 1980 and from the Mid-America College of Funeral Service in 1983. He became a licensed funeral director and embalmer in Kentucky in 1984 and then became a Qualified Mortuary Disaster Coordinator for the Commonwealth of Kentucky in 1987. He is a member of the Funeral Directors Association of Kentucky and the National Funeral Directors Association, and he as served in various public positions and on boards across the years. He is also a former coach, board member, and game official of Little League Basketball and Baseball and of Babe Ruth Baseball for over twenty years.

William Lee Shannon

A fourth-generation funeral director, William Lee Shannon was born April 25, 1919, in Shelbyville. His parents lived in an apartment over the Shannon Undertaking Company, which included a casket selection room, a small hallway, a preparation room, and a small office.

Shannon attended Washington and Lee University for four years and later attended the Melton School of Mortuary Science (later the Kentucky School of Mortuary Science), located on West Broadway in Louisville. He married his girlfriend of four years the day after he graduated in 1946, and the couple went back to Shelbyville, where Shannon "naturally fell right into the funeral business" as a licensed funeral director. Shannon taught at his alma mater for twenty-five years on a part-time basis, from 1946 until 1971.

Shannon notes that his great-grandfather started the first family funeral business in 1865 in LaGrange, Kentucky. Shannon's grandfather went into the business too but moved to Shelbyville in 1899.

Julius M. Steele Jr.

Julius M. Steele Jr., known as Jay, was born August 6, 1952, in Hazard. Upon completing high school, he served an apprenticeship from 1971 to 1973 at the Engle Funeral Home in Hazard. He graduated from the Kentucky School of Mortuary Science, Louisville, in August 1974 and received the Bill Pierce Award for the most professional attitude toward funeral service.

While attending mortuary school, Steele began working at the Buchanan Funeral Home, and he continued there until 1978. He was then funeral director and embalmer for four years at the Kilgore Collier Funeral Home, Catlettsburg, and for two additional years at funeral homes in Bardwell and Wickliffe. From 1984 to 1987, Steele lived in Seymour, Indiana, where he did not work in funeral service. He moved to Pineville in May 1987, and became owner of the Arnett and Steele Funeral Home. He continues to work there and is involved with many funeral service organizations and community groups. Steele's wife, Mary, and their son, Jason, are also funeral directors and embalmers and work in the family business. Their daughter, Margaret Mary Steele, works in the Southwest Louisiana Crime Lab in Lake Charles.

Charles Strode

Born August 28, 1938, in Tompkinsville, Charles Strode decided in seventh grade that he wanted a career in the funeral business. At seventeen, he worked briefly at the G. H. Herman Funeral Home in Indianapolis. He then returned to Tompkinsville to work for John Ed Yokley, and later for Don Butler, at the Yokley Funeral Home. Strode and his wife, Dixie, moved to Shelbyville, where he worked for the Hall-Tater Funeral Home for about eighteen months, but they returned to Tompkinsville in 1966 to open the Strode-Lyons Funeral Home with business partner Glenn Lyons.

In 1972, the Strodes purchased the rest of the business from the Lyons family and renamed it the Strode Funeral Home. Since the death of his wife, Strode has operated the funeral home with his daughter, Charlotte, a funeral director and high school teacher, as his partner. She and her husband, Dr. Stephen Birge, have a son and a daughter in school.

Strode served Monroe County as elected county coroner for nearly thirty years but resigned when Governor Paul Patton appointed him to the Kentucky Board of Embalmers and Funeral Directors. Strode has been on the board for thirteen years and now serves as chair. Previously he was president of the Funeral Directors Association of Kentucky.

Gregory Woodruff

Gregory Ray Woodruff was born January 24, 1961, in Madisonville. He is the first person in his family to be involved in the funeral business, fulfilling a dream his father had but was unable to pursue. Woodruff started his funeral service career in 1979 in Salem, his adopted hometown, where he and his wife, Charlene, still reside. In 1983 he graduated from the Mid-America College of Funeral Service, Jeffersonville, Indiana, and acquired his funeral director and embalmer licenses.

In 2006 Woodruff purchased a small funeral home in Symsonia, Graves County, known as Funeral Service Directors, which he currently operates. His hobbies include collecting funeral-related comics, funeral home memorabilia, darkroom photography, and remote-control airplanes.

CPSIA information can be obtained
at www.ICGtesting.com
Printed in the USA
FFHW021528120919
54914878-60630FF